The Manifesto is not "find the pain," it's...

Find the pleasure, make the sale, and build the relati...

JEFFREY GITOMER'S

SALES MANIFESTO

Imperative Actions You Need to Take and Master to Dominate Your Competition and Win For Yourself…For The Next Decade.

Jeffrey Gitomer's Sales Manifesto
© Copyright 2019 by Jeffrey Gitomer, Gitgo LLC.

Published by Sound Wisdom 717-530-2122. Info@soundwisdom.com

For more information on distribution call 717-530-2122 or info@soundwisdom.com. For bulk sales discounts, call our friendly office 704-333-1112 or email helpme@gitomer.com

The author may be contacted at salesman@gitomer.com
Websites: www.gitomer.com, www.GitomerLearningAcademy.com

Edited by Jennifer Gluckow.
Page design by Mike Wolff.
Cover design by Ashley Gadd.

Printed in the United States by RR Donnelley
Second Printing, February 2019

Library of Congress Control Number: 2018954722
Gitomer, Jeffrey
Jeffrey Gitomer's Sales Manifesto: Imperative Actions You Need to Take and Master to Dominate Your Competition and Win for Yourself...For the Next Decade
ISBN-10: 0-999255-52-5
ISBN-13: 978-0-999255-52-0

If you want to build wealth, first build a wealth of knowledge.

Jeffrey Gitomer
KING of SALES

JEFFREY GITOMER'S
SALES MANIFESTO
Table of Contents

MISSION 1 – UNDERSTANDING MANIFESTO

MISSION 2 – THE MANIFESTO SALE

MISSION 3 – MANIFESTO PRINCIPLES

MISSION 4 – MANIFESTO STRATEGIES

MISSION 5 – MANIFESTO MASTERY

You learn by clarification
of situation and opportunity.
You become proficient
by taking action.
You master by repetition
of process.

Jeffrey Gitomer
KING of SALES

Weak salespeople look at quotas and become fearful. Mediocre salespeople look at quotas as a goal. Manifesto salespeople look at quotas and laugh.

Jeffrey Gitomer
KING of SALES

Understanding Manifesto

People will rain on your parade
because they have no parade
of their own.

Jeffrey Gitomer
KING of SALES

(The old way of selling doesn't work anymore) it's no longer... it's now all about...

The old way of selling is dead.
Here's why, and how to master the new
way to dominate your market,
destroy your competition,
make the sale, and get your price.

For decades, the model and philosophy around the selling process has focused on a model of "prospecting, presenting, overcoming objections, and closing the sale." This process causes manipulation, bidding, price comparison, and ultimate frustration among salespeople and sales leaders due to loss of profit even if the sale is won.

Clearly a new model and a new strategy is needed – a better sales model without manipulation, and one that leads to a trusted, non-bidding, profitable relationship. One where the customer buys based on the value perceived, not just price. One that includes social involvement and engagement. And one that can continue to grow as the salesperson progresses.

This new model changes the game and brings you permanently into the 21st century.

It combines face-to-face, online, social media, and social selling. This one book will shape you and make you for the next decade. Not just more sales and more money. It will make you a better salesperson and a better person. In short – it's not just how to make a sale. *The Manifesto Sale* will help you build relationships that lead to referrals.

The new approach takes on an entirely different view of how the sale is prepared for and how the sale is COMPLETED, not closed. It places a new and powerful set of criteria for the salesperson for connecting and building relationships that, once implemented, leads to improved skills, improved sales, improved reputation, and improved profits.

Here's a brief explanation of what's in store as you read, watch, learn, and implement:

The Manifesto Sale identifies in simple language the 6.5 parts of the new sale, and builds easy-to-learn and easy-to-implement models for each component:

1. **Value Attraction** (creating social messages that make the reader/viewer/listener want more)

2. **THEM Preparation** (planning strategy, getting ready, and executing in terms of the customer)

3. **Value Engagement** (attraction PLUS value equals connection)

4. **Connection and Completion** (perceived value beyond price in both "how to connect" and "connect to make a sale")

5. **Building profitable long-term relationships** (loyal, value-driven customers)

6. **Building a permanent referable first-class reputation** (both online and community based)

6.5 **Executing the Non-System of Selling** (the only thing this non-system is NOT is manipulation)

Let me describe the steps a bit more in depth...

Part one: Attraction is a combination of social outreach and branding. It's consistent messages and offerings in favor of the recipient that are so well received that they're shared, forwarded, posted, and re-tweeted to the followers of the seller.

Part two: Preparation offers a new model that identifies and defines (1) the situation, (2) the opportunities, (3) the objectives, and (4) the outcome, ALL IN FAVOR OF THE CUSTOMER – and challenges you that part (4.5) the glue that holds the rest of getting ready together, is: BEST. Doing your best at ALL TIMES ensures a higher percentage of favorable outcomes.

Part three: Engagement is a 4.5 part scenario that has built-in value to every offering. (1) Why would a prospective customer be engaged by your words? (2) Why would a prospective customer be engaged by your offer? (3) What is the prospective customer's perception of the difference between you and your competition? (4) How easy does the customer perceive it is to do business with you? (4.5) The engagement messages must be both valuable to the reader and consistent in their offering. That's the formula that enables a profitable connection process to take place.

Part four: Connecting identifies traditional networking connection opportunities, COMBINED with a business social media outreach to attract the best possible contacts and prospects through the following sources: (1) unsolicited referrals, (2) social media attraction, engagement, and connection, (3) existing customers, and (4) networking connections.

And teaches you how you can provide a consistent value message in favor of the customer so that they STAY connected and are loyal. The glue in the entire connection process is value and reputation – both online and word-of-mouth.

Part five: Building Profitable Relationships and it challenges the new model of selling salesperson that service and value after the sale leads to loyalty. And loyalty leads to repeat business and referrals. Detail is offered on how relationships are built and maintained over time, and how relationships also help drive profits and eliminate competition.

Part six: Reputation – is the strength of character that arrives to the sale way before the salesperson does. It focuses on the missed opportunity to build personal brand and credibility that can spell the difference between sale and no sale.

And, part 6.5 is Executing. Like customer engagement and connection, it contains the fundamental and foundational steps to the NEW sale. I refer to it as: The Non-System of Selling – intelligent, emotional, friendly, value-driven engagement. The steps are: (1) the questions you ask, (2) the ideas you present, (3) your compelling presentation skills, (4) your perceived difference, your perceived value, and your proof, and (4.5) the glue that holds the rest of executing together is the attitude, belief, and enthusiasm you are able to transfer to the prospect or customer.

Until you wake up to the reality that the old way of selling doesn't work anymore, you are as doomed as the fax machine, the blackberry, and the yellow pages.

- **Saving money versus making a profit.** CEOs and CFOs want to make a profit. They are not interested in saving money. The only people interested in saving money are purchasing agents and other lower level employees trying to look good and take away your profit. Start at the top.

- **Transitioning from alone to not alone.** Who is with you when you make a sale? If you want to meet with the potential customer's CEO, bring yours and arrange a meeting. I promise you the sale will go faster and smoother.

- **Everyone wants PROOF.** What is with you when you make a sale? When you say things about yourself it's bragging. When you bring video testimonials of other customers corroborating your story and your statements, it's PROOF!

- **Who is referring you?** This is the ultimate MANIFESTO REPORT CARD. If customers are proactively giving you referrals – without you asking – then you have done everything plus more than was expected of you. If you're looking for a measuring device, unsolicited referrals is the tool.

MANIFESTO DEFINED...

MANIFESTO is not just MORE.
MANIFESTO is ACTION.
Think. Read. Experience. Observe.
Collect – ideas and friends.
Expose your thoughts.
Attract. Prepare and Be Prepared.
Internet. Intend. Engage. Relate.
Differentiate. Prove value.
Serve with pride. Stay humble.
Stay sober.
Write. Post. Respond.
Love it or leave it.
Reward – yourself and others.
Do the right thing all the time.

Jeffrey Gitomer

There is no prize for second place in sales You either win or lose – that's it.

Every economic indicator and every economist is predicting BOOM.

I believe we're in for a ten-year amazing run of prosperity.

The only question is: HOW WILL YOU PROSPER?

This book has sales answers of certainty.

I think the annual issues and challenges of "achieve all your goals," "have your best year ever," and other variations of that process are pretty much played out.

Of course you want to achieve your goals, of course you want to have your best year ever, or do you? This book is about having your best DECADE ever! The question is: how do you make that happen? Or better stated how do you make that happen at your level at this moment?

This book is not just the "how-to" – it's a no bullshit book of ANSWERS and ACTIONS that will put you on top of your sales world and keep you there.

What is a sales manifesto?

A sales manifesto is a series of directives and answers that lead to real world success.
No theory. No fluff. No bullshit.
Just sales and facts.

How do I benefit from this book?

This is a book of sales ideas and answers you can use the minute you learn them.

This book will inspire you and give you confidence to take new actions and make more sales.

How do I use this book to succeed and build wealth?

This is a book of sales imperatives.

This is a book of next generation sales and personal development directives and strategies you can use **TODAY.**

This is the sales book that all other sales books will use as a benchmark.

What is "disruption"?

The secret of my sales success... I'm disruptive.

Disruption goes against the grain of conventional and traditional thinking, and causes the marketplace to reconsider their goals and objectives.

Disruption changes the norm. Disruption separates you from the mediocre.

It's against the wind where there are few travelers, and it's upstream – where the fish are.

I have been disruptive for the past 30 years.

My sales perspective – soon your perspective – flies in the face of traditional selling.

Cold calling, find the pain, pitch the product, close the sale, customer satisfaction are all total bullshit.

These are my GENUINE disruptive MANIFESTO elements that will lead you to the NEW SALE...

- **Value attraction**

- **Social attraction**

- **Find the pleasure**

- **Ask emotional questions**

- **Discover the motive to buy**

- **Offer IDEAS not a sales pitch**

- **Confirm the urgency of the offer**

- **Give before and after the sale value**

- **Earn customer loyalty**

- **Earn referrals**

These elements are not "rocket science" rather they are ROCKET FUEL. Fuel to propel you to sales success. Each element is fully explained throughout this book. And these are just the beginning.

This SALES MANIFESTO is yours for the taking, the learning, the understanding, the implementing, and the banking.

The Manifesto Sale

People don't like to be sold,
but they love to BUY!™

Jeffrey Gitomer
KING of SALES

FULL TABLE OF MANIFESTO ELEMENTS AND ACTIONS

These ELEMENTS AND ACTIONS are transitions you must master to go from what is no longer valid in sales to...

THE MANIFESTO SALE

The MANIFESTO Sale

- **It's no longer selling. It's all about the customer buying.** People don't like to be sold but they love to buy™, is my registered trademark and my lifelong sales philosophy. As the rules of sales change, this one rule stays as a benchmark sales strategy – and it is THE MOST VIOLATED of all selling strategies.

- **It's no longer the salesperson bragging. It's all about video proof.** Social proof is now the new norm. People posting videos on every form of social media in favor of or against the people they did business with. Those videos create reputation, reality, and the future of the company's sales.

- **It's no longer scripts, it's about customized and personalized presentations.** Scripting sounds like insincere jargon. The customer wants customized presentation. IT'S ALL ABOUT THEM.

- **It's no longer a presentation. It's all about your performance.** Think about your sales presentation. Now think about singing a song. Both require audience approval and acceptance to win. SING BABY.

- **It's no longer manipulation. It's all about harmonizing.** The old way of selling is dead. Meaningful dialog, social engagement, and value messages have replaced manipulative selling forever.

- **It's no longer body language. It's about common ground and rapport.** SALES MANIFESTO experts don't try to "read" the situation, they create the situation, AND THE OUTCOME.

- **It's no longer cold-calling. It's all about relationships and referrals.** Cold calling is a sales strategy, but by execution, the hardest, and by successful percentage of successful outcome, THE LOWEST. Think: Socially connecting. Think: Referrals.

- **It's no longer a sales pitch. It's about helping the customer win.** If your slide deck does not show the customer how they win, how they make a profit, and how they produce more from owning your product or service, then ditch your presentation in favor of one that helps customers.

- **It's no longer closing a sale. It's all about opening (THEN gaining commitment).** If it doesn't start right, it will never end right. The key to closing the sale is in direct proportion to how well the sale opens.

- **It's no longer selling your product. It's all about outcome after purchase.** Don't focus on selling, Focus on what happens after the customer takes ownership. Making the sale is easy, making certain the outcome exceeds the customer's expectation creates the relationship.

- **It's no longer low-level non-decision-makers. It's all about the CEO.** If you start at the top, working with people at the bottom becomes a hell of a lot easier. If you start at the bottom, getting to the top is often impossible.

- **It's no longer about follow up. It's all about follow through.** Following up is merely a call asking for money. Following through makes certain that you close the sale, deliver the product, and creates a positive outcome. Follow-up is old world. Follow-through is MANIFESTO SELLING.

- **It's no longer being a great salesperson. It's about becoming a trusted advisor.** You gain trust by giving trust. You can only become a trusted advisor by being a trustworthy person.

- **It's no longer you calling the customer. It's all about the customer calling you.** Create reasons and opportunities for the customer to call you. Consistent posts, great reputation, memorable service, speak in public, community visibility, active civic participation at a leadership level.

- **It's no longer the "law of attraction." It's all about "value attraction." Value attraction is one of the fulcrum elements of manifesto selling.** You create value attraction by posting consistent messages that your customer PERCEIVES as valuable. More than the "law of attraction," you must create your own attraction.

- **It's no longer price. It's all about PERCEIVED VALUE.** When YOU are making a purchase, if the value exceeds the price, you will buy. The same goes for your customer. 74% of customers will buy value over price.

The MANIFESTO Social Sale

- **It's no longer website bragging. It's all about business social media as social proof.** The percentage of brag-to-proof should be: 1 brag post to every 5 proof posts. Fix your ratio fast and sales will rise.

- **It's no longer salespeople bragging. It's all about social proof.** Think about how valuable and important testimonials are. Now think about how few testimonials you have. Create a MANIFESTO plan to earn (get) more social proof.

- **It's no longer you Googling the customer. It's all about the customer Googling you.** Google yourself RIGHT NOW. That is what your customer sees as he or she is talking to you on the phone, or as you enter their office. GET GOOGLE-ABLE. Your Google results are the MANIFESTATION of your MANIFESTO.

- **It's no longer just advertising. It's all about word-of-mouth AND word-of-mouse advertising.** What people say and post about you is one million times more powerful than your ad in the paper.

- **It's no longer brochures. It's all about blogging and posting real stories.** "Once upon a time…" is much more appealing to readers than "we are the greatest." Tell the story THEN make the point.

- **It's no longer being liked on Facebook. It's all about being LIVE on Facebook.** Regardless of your political feelings about Facebook, the reality is they are the largest country in the world. You may want to begin to take advantage of the feature that allows you to go live, and broadcast to the world. I have started doing it and can report my findings in two words: IT WORKS!

- **It's no longer desktop. It's all about mobile.** You can easily do without your laptop or desktop for a day or two, but you cannot do without your phone for a minute, let alone two minutes. Your smartphone connects you to the world and all of its information and resources. It's also your main tool to connect with customers by social media, email, and text. Don't just "use" your phone, become the master of it.

- **It's no longer internet. It's all about app.** Apps are now more utilized than the Internet. That's a reality that tells you where sales are going and growing. Got app? Consider an app that's both fun and addictive.

We have chosen to go the way of the "game." Our sales and personal development games teach by repetition, and the app itself creates competition for all who play. It's the perfect sales storm (go to www.GitomerLearningAcademy.com for a preview).

- **It's no longer just posting text. It's all about having your own PODCAST.** I am using our Podcast as a means to connect with my audience, reach new potential subscribers and customers, and keep my message consistently broadcast over the Internet and smartphone. Podcasting is growing exponentially, and the new leaders will emerge by the spoken word more than by the written word. For me personally, I have chosen to stay with both. My partner Jennifer Gluckow and I now do our SELL or DIE podcast daily, and we have reached more than 100,000 downloads a month to prove my point, BUT I still write and post every day. I believe "podcast plus post" to be the strongest promotional combination.

- **It's no longer just being interviewed. It's all about being a guest on a PODCAST.** Search for podcasts in your area of expertise. Connect and request to be a guest. Go prepared. If you're good, you'll get all kinds of responses. ALL POSITIVE. FOR FREE. Being a podcast guest simultaneously increases your visibility and authenticity.

- **It's no longer email addresses. It's all about cell phone numbers.** If you are able to get your prospect's or your customer's cell phone number, it tells you that you are trusted enough to text. Texting is now the instant response mechanism that the fax machine was 30 years ago. Everyone looks at their texts immediately. If you get it, don't abuse it.

- **It's no longer who you know. It's all about who knows you.** You don't have to fight for recognition, all you have to do is earn it. You earn it by being valuable, you earn it by posting consistent valuable messages, and you earn it by the reputation you've achieved when someone Googles your name. When you become valuable you never have to justify you are again. You can start higher when you make a sales call, and you have credibility before you begin.

- **It's no longer cold-calling. It's all about LinkedIn.** Take ONE MINUTE before you make your next cold call and find your prospect on LinkedIn. Connect with him or her, and send them a link to your one-page website. Jot down a question or two to prepare, THEN CALL. Your results will amaze you.

- **It's no longer tweeting. It's all about being re-tweeted.** Most salespeople and business people are twitter weak. Don't be that person. Get my ReTweet-ables free e-book (www.buygitomer.com/products/retweetables), follow the instructions, and begin to get re-tweeted.

- **It's no longer just written text. It's all about spoken word and video.** The sales monopoly game has changed for the better. People are no longer passing go and collecting $200. They are passing viral messages and collecting millions. Don't just watch and listen, participate (and collect)!

- **It's no longer written testimonials. It's all about your customer posting Facebook testimonial videos, Instagram stories, and proof on your YouTube channel.** Social media and social sales is ruled by the customer. Their rating, their service response, their posting, and their stories have become the new norm. People will believe those videos and those postings and purchase accordingly (or not). The only way to secure these golden pieces of testimony is to EARN THEM!

- **It's no longer trolling for leads on LinkedIn. It's posting value messages and having LinkedIn prospects ask you to connect.** If you are not posting consistent value messages on LinkedIn and your other social platforms, then you will be relegated to searching LinkedIn for potential customers and being looked upon as a troll. Not good. The more value you post, aimed at the people you want to connect with, the easier it's going to be for them to want more from you.

The MANIFESTO Customer Service and Loyalty

- **It's no longer about customer satisfaction. It's all about customer loyalty.** Customer satisfaction is the most bogus measurement ever placed in the mind of a customer. I want loyalty, not satisfaction. The measurement of success with your customer in your company boils down to two things:

  1. Will you do business with me again?

  2. Will you refer me?

  All other measurements are bogus and worthless. If you want proof, take the JD power customer satisfaction award: they give it to airlines! What could the category possibly be?

- **It's no longer customer service. It's all about helping the customer succeed in their business.** Merely providing service to your customers does not ensure loyalty or reorders. You must be a value provider, and someone the customer can count on to help improve THEIR business.

- **It's no longer great service. It's about being memorable.** In today's world of "instant service," "easy returns," and "online ratings," the only service that rules is "memorable service." Memorable is the "Plus 1" offered AFTER service takes place.

- **It's no longer a computer answering the phone. It's all about answering live.** "To serve you better please select from among the following nine options," is not only a lie, it's an insult. Even large companies are getting back to saying hello and answering the phone with a live human being. 24-7 answering services are all over the planet. Hire one. Mine is www.bcanswer.com.

- **It's no longer a transaction. It's an opportunity to earn respect and a relationship.** Every sale and every service call is an additional sales opportunity. Unfortunately many people who serve customers look at customer interactions as a distraction. Serve to sell again. Serve to dominate. Serve to rule.

Be Prepared Re-defined

- **It's no longer your sales pitch. It's all about your creativity.** What's the difference between you and your competitor? That's what your customer is wanting to know. If you walk in with a creative presentation, that's a good start. If you can engage them emotionally, that's the next step. And if you can give ideas that the customer perceives as valuable, and back it up with some form of proof, you will win the sale at your price. Otherwise it's a sales pitch that ends with: "Can you please send me a proposal?"

- **It's no longer a marketing-prepared/canned presentation. It's about preparing in terms of the customer.** When you walk in with a deck of slides, and information about you and your product, you are totally unprepared to make a sale. The customer is expecting intelligent and engaging questions, knowledge about them and their issues, and an idea or two to help differentiate you from your competitor. Slides lose. Ideas rule.

- **It's no longer presenting facts. It's about bringing ideas to the conversation.** As you can see from this list, I am a huge proponent of bringing ideas that favor the customer into the sales call. That's the manifesto way. Your prospect will listen to your idea a thousand times more than they will listen to your presentation.

- **It's no longer telling. It's about asking powerful, emotionally engaging questions.** When you are talking, you're not learning. Learning about the customer's needs, wants, motives, and expected outcomes. That's where the sale is. Stop talking and start asking, and your sales will double.

You Re-defined

- **It's no longer watching television. It's all about writing and personal branding.** More than a waste of time, TV is a waste of life. The best way to justify watching anything on television is ask yourself: Will watching this show double my income? If it won't, you might want to reconsider *investing* your time on something that will both earn money and create legacy. While you are watching television, I'm writing books. It's a choice.

- **It's no longer time management. It's all about time allocation.** Managing time is an impossibility. Allocating time will triple productivity and at the same time put you on a path to greater earnings. Allocate your time in 30-minute chunks, and watch the unbelievable results.

- **It's no longer Googling the customer. It's all about the customer Googling you.** Salespeople use Google to research prospective customers, never once realizing that the customer is Googling them. Challenge: GOOGLE YOURSELF RIGHT NOW. That's what your customer sees as you enter the sales call. Start your MANIFESTO journey by fixing that.

- **It's no longer proficiency. It's all about mastery.** In order to succeed in today's sales world you have to be a sales master. Not just at selling skills, also attitude, writing, listening, relationship building, and value offerings. If you are only slightly better than your competitor, it's likely you will lose as often as you win. Invest the time it takes to get to mastery. The price you will pay is small compared to the amount you will win.

- **It's no longer knowing. It's all about understanding and applying.** Salespeople think they know everything, but the problem is they don't do it. There's a difference between knowing and doing. Between knowing and applying. The difference is winning and money.

- **It's no longer goals and goal setting. It's all about intentions and achievement.** If I had $0.25 for every goal that was set but not achieved, I would be a multibillionaire. Goals without intentions are worthless. Anything you set your mind to do, must be committed to, intended to, and dedicated to achieve. The secret of goals is not setting them, it's intending to achieve them, and committing to a deadline. Just do it.

- **It's no longer being an example. It's all about setting the standard.** If you look at today's billionaires and maximum achievers, not one of them leads by example. Every one of them sets the standard. The standard for others to follow. If you're looking to be the manifesto salesperson that you're hoping to become, setting the standard is the only way to get there.

- **It's no longer about the company's reputation. It's about YOUR reputation.** When you Google yourself, you uncover what your customer sees as they make the determination of who you are as a person. Also known as your "reputation," the elements and postings of Google create an image in the mind of your customer as to who they are dealing with. Not your company, not your product, YOU! My strongest recommendation is that you Google yourself to understand where you are right now, and make a game plan to build your online reputation to a point of "impressive."

- **It's no longer comparing to the competition. It's about being perceived as different FROM the competition.**
  This is a very simple explanation: when you compare yourself to your competitor, it's a price comparison. When you differentiate yourself FROM your competition, it's based on value. What is your value, stated in a way that your customer perceives it as valuable and makes a buying decision in your favor. Differentiate, NOT compare. Value NOT price. Simple.

- **It's no longer hating the competition. It's all about the competition hating you.** If you hate your competition it means that they are beating you. If they hate you, it means that you are beating them.

- **It's no longer money. It's all about wealth.** Wealth comes in many forms. Of course money is the easiest one to measure, but you can have wealth in the form of: your family, your library, your writing, travel experiences, and your knowledge. Never measure wealth in terms of money alone. Oftentimes it's the least important part.

- **It's no longer success. It's all about fulfillment.** Just because you're successful does not mean you are fulfilled. Success is not only defined by money. It is defined by happiness, health, family, and the feeling that you have achieved what you set out to achieve.

CHALLENGE: I just presented you a list of manifesto transitions. As mind-boggling as they first appear to be, the mountain is not so tall that you can't climb it, and put your flag in at the top.

Manifesto Moment

The Manifesto Sale focuses on the customer, is value based, contains zero manipulation, is easily understood, creates real attraction, and provides salespeople with the one thing they're hoping for as they progress up the ladder of success: IMPLEMENTABLE ANSWERS.

The Manifesto Sale is the only way.

*To achieve the best I can be for myself, my customers,
and my company these are my…*

22.5 Sales Manifesto Commandments

1. I am going to act like every day is my first day on the job. I will impress everyone.

2. I treat every customer as though they were Michael Jordan.

3. The customer I'm speaking to now is the most important person on earth.

4. I smile all the time.

5. My job/career depends on the way I treat customers.

6. I set the tone. I will make it a positive one.

7. I'm friendly, enthusiastic, and positive. Three of the most powerful action words in the world.

8. I start with "YES."

9. It's not just what I say, it's how I say it.

10. I'm excited for the customer.

11. I understand that customers buy for their reasons, not mine. I will find out their reasons – first.

12. I understand that people have other problems besides what I sell.

13. One of my goals is to make, "I'll handle it personally," a way of life.

14. I call customers by name.

15. I help people get what they want.

16. Even though it's my 10,000th time, it's their first.

17. I will ask for the sale.

18. My goals are posted where I can see them all the time.

19. I record myself every week, and listen for one hour.

20. I spend 20 minutes a day learning something new.

21. I know our product like I know my name.

22. I'm doing my BEST – all the time.

22.5 I thank everyone for everything every time.

16.5 Manifesto Sales Elements

Jeffrey Gitomer's 16.5 Commandments of MASTERING Sales Success

1. People don't like to be sold, but they love to buy™. Find out why people want to buy and you will become the Manifesto Master.

2. The first sale that's made is the salesperson. If they don't buy you, they won'y buy anything you're selling.

3. Your reputation arrives before you do. Google and word-of-mouth determine your fate way before you start talking.

4. Get interesting. This will overcome one of the top ten sales objections: "Not Interested!"

5. People buy for their reasons not yours. Find out their reasons BEFORE you start your presentation.

6. Your questions make or break you. Ask engaging, emotional questions to get to the heart of the sale.

7. Ideas win – slide decks lose. If you bring an idea in favor of the customer, it will make your slide deck unnecessary.

8. You must be able to transfer "The Knowledge."* To transfer "The Knowledge," prospects and customers need to feel your

passion – your belief – your intelligence – your ideas – and your sincerity beyond the hype of your sales pitch.
*"The Knowledge" is the certification for a London taxi driver. To get a full license he or she must know the city like the back of his/her hand. It takes 4 years. Same with your knowledge.

9. PROVE IT! Testimonials sell where salespeople cannot. When you say things about yourself, it's bragging. What people say about you is proof!

10. All things being equal, people want to do business with their friends. Got friends?

11. Networking works. Targeted Networking, face-to-face, leads to connections, appointments, presentations, and sales.

12. It starts with LIKE. If they like you, and they believe you, and they have confidence in you and they trust you, then they MAY buy from you.

13. Find THEIR "why." It's not about how to sell, it's about why they buy.

14. Sell to help and commissions just show up. Change commission thinking to mission thinking.

15. It's NOT satisfaction, it's LOYALTY. *Loyalty defined:* Will you do business with me again? Will you refer me?

16. Ask for the sale every time. Why wouldn't you ask for the sale every time? Why don't YOU ask for the sale every time?

16.5 HERE'S the SECRET. It's hard work. **HERE'S the BIGGER SECRET:** Most salespeople are not willing to do the hard work it takes that makes selling easy.

Words of SUCCESS, and WEALTH CAUTION...
If there are shortcuts to success and wealth, please send them to me – I have never been able to find one. Take the LONG CUT. And, cut the things out of your life that waste time, aren't important or aren't making you money.

Jeffrey Gitomer

Out of touch or out of their minds? Maybe both!

In a survey conducted by a BIG benefits management company (a management and human resource consulting firm), they asked 365 CEOs and sales management executives, "What are the three key factors that separate high performing sales professionals from moderate to low performing sales professionals?"

Both CEOs and C-level sales executives (all people who don't sell, but rely on their salespeople to produce sales so that they can get paid), ranked "self discipline/motivation" as the most important.

Next in line were, "customer knowledge," "innate talent/ personality," "product knowledge," and further down the list were "experience" and "teamwork skills."

Totally bogus.

These are qualities of corporate greed. Value, service, and help are the REAL three things that customers require to give their business and maintain their loyalty.

MAJOR DUH: When "survey" companies ask questions of people, why don't they ask the people actually doing the work?

I'm a writer, but I'm also a salesman. I make sales calls and sales every day. If you're interested in the most important factors of a high-performing salesperson, let me give you a realistic list of success characteristics.

1. Perpetual, consistent, positive attitude and enthusiasm. This is the first rule of facing the customer, facing the obstacles, facing the competition, facing the economy, and facing yourself. Especially the people that answer the phone.

2. Quadruple self-belief. Unwavering belief in your company; unwavering belief in your product; AND unwavering belief in yourself are the first three rules. But fourth is the most critical of the self-beliefs. You MUST believe that the customer is better off having purchased from you.

3. Use of creativity. Creativity to present ideas in favor of the customer, and creativity to differentiate you from the competition.

4. Ability to give and prove value. Prove the value of your product or service, and give value beyond the sale to the PROSPECT so you can earn the order, the reorder and the loyalty.

5. Ability to promote and position. Personal use of the internet to blog, web, post, email magazine, utilize social media, and achieve reputation through Google top ranking, so your customers and prospects will perceive you as a value provider and a leader in your field.

6. Exciting, compelling presentation skills. Not just solid communication skills, but superior questioning skills, listening skills and a sense of humor. The innate ability to engage and capture the imagination (and the wallet) of customers and prospects.

7. The ability to "click" face-to-face. Finding common ground in order to relax the conversation and use rapport to get to truth.

8. Ability to prove your value and claims through the testimony of others. Testimonials sell where salespeople can't. The BEST salespeople use video testimonials on YouTube to support, affirm, and prove their claims. BUT, the reality is – you don't get testimonials, you EARN them. (Same with referrals.)

NOTE WELL: *If you're looking for proof that you are "top-performing," testimonials and referrals are a report card.*

9. Ability to create an atmosphere where people want to BUY (because they hate being SOLD). This is done by engaging and asking. Not presenting and telling.

10. Ability to build a relationship, not hunt or farm. I wonder if the "executives" talking about the factors of great salespeople are the same morons dividing their salespeople into "hunters" and "farmers." PLEASE HELP ME. Great salespeople are relationship builders who provide value and help their customers win. These are the same head-in-the-sand executives that can't open their laptops, and forbid Facebook at work, individual websites, and blogs from their people. ADVICE: If this is your situation, find your way to the competition.

11. A PERSONAL social media platform that promotes your social selling and builds your reputation. The minimums are: 1,000 business Facebook likes, 501 LinkedIn connections, 500 Twitter followers, 25 YouTube videos, and a blog where you post weekly.

12. Unyielding personal values and ethics. Great people have great values and great ethics. Interesting that 365 CEOs and executives don't deem them in the top ten.

12.5 The personal desire to excel and be their best. This is a desired quality of every salesperson, BUT the best salespeople have mastered the other twelve elements. They must be mastered in order for this quality to manifest itself.

There is no prize in sales for second place. It's win or nothing. The masters know this, and strive for, fight for, that slight edge.

And as for the next poll taken, here's a great idea for CEOs and sales executives. There's an easy way to find out the most important factors and qualities of great salespeople: make some sales calls yourself.

And if you really want to have some fun, bring your marketing people along.

All things being equal, people want to do business with their friends. All things being not quite so equal, people still want to do business with their friends.

Jeffrey Gitomer
KING of SALES

The 17.5 questions were the easy part. Here's the MANIFESTO part. The 17.5 **statements** you must rate yourself on to prove your own manifesto Mindset.

HOW TO SCORE: Circle the number that corresponds to your present situation, feeling, or skill level.

(1=poor, 2=average, 3=good, 4=very good, 5=the greatest)
(1=never, 2=rarely, 3=sometimes, 4=frequently, 5=all the time/daily)

❏ I am willing to do my BEST every day.   **1 2 3 4 5**

❏ I love what I do enough to do my BEST every day.   **1 2 3 4 5**

❏ I believe in myself.   **1 2 3 4 5**

❏ I am a daily student of sales, attitude, value, and life.   **1 2 3 4 5**

❏ I read enough to learn new things.   **1 2 3 4 5**

❏ I write enough value messages to post and create attraction.   **1 2 3 4 5**

❏ My attitude is as positive as it can be.   **1 2 3 4 5**

❏ I have the genuine desire to achieve at this career.   **1 2 3 4 5**

❐ I am dedicated to making my own
success a reality.   **1 2 3 4 5**

❐ I believe I can overcome/eliminate the
barriers holding me back.   **1 2 3 4 5**

❐ I help others without expectation of return. **1 2 3 4 5**

❐ I build solid long-term relationships.   **1 2 3 4 5**

❐ I have the connections and relationships
I need to build my career.   **1 2 3 4 5**

❐ I spend my time with the type of people
I want to become.   **1 2 3 4 5**

❐ I am honorable in all my dealings.   **1 2 3 4 5**

❐ I am considered a trusted advisor by others. **1 2 3 4 5**

❐ I am proud of what comes up when
I Google myself.   **1 2 3 4 5**

❐ I proudly tell my mom about everything
I do.   **1 2 3 4 5**

How to Personalize the Test

There are 18 total statements. Go back and review your
answers. Check the boxes on the left where you scored 1, 2,
or 3. Those are your weak areas. The checked boxes become
your personalized game plan to get a better manifesto
mindset. Now all you have to do is take daily positive action
on one or more of your self-ratings. More helpful ideas,
strategies and answers are on the pages that follow.

Jeffrey Gitomer's KEY Behaviors of Top Sales MANIFESTO Producers

- Yes! Attitude

- Deep belief in yourself and your ability to help others

- Value provider – able to get a fair, profitable price

- Able to transfer his or her message

- Authentic, ethical, honest, friendly, believable, and trustworthy

- Nano-second responsiveness

- Kept promises

- Persuasive, NOT pushy

- Assertive, NOT aggressive

- Follow through, NOT just follow up

- Offer quality product and service

- Easy to do business with

- Impeccable reputation – others willing to speak for him/her

- Relationship driven, NOT quota driven, NOT transactional

- Has and displays character and confidence – resilient

- Socially viable and valuable

- Connectable and personally responsible

- Able to find and meet with the decision-maker

- Delivers on every promise – reliable

- Trusted as a person and a provider

- Have a 4x pipeline – never force an "end of the month" sale

- Takes actions to become referable

- Mission driven, NOT commission driven

Manifesto Moment

It's Mission Thinking, NOT Commission Thinking

You just looked at the KEY BEHAVIORS of OTHERS.
Let's see how you rate yourself on the behaviors you
must master to prove your own MANIFESTO capability.

HOW TO SCORE: Circle the number that corresponds to your
present situation, feeling, or skill level

(1=poor, 2=average, 3=good, 4=very good, 5=the greatest)
(1=never, 2=rarely, 3=sometimes, 4=frequently,
5=all the time/daily)

❏ I have a YES! Attitude. **1 2 3 4 5**

❏ I have a deep belief in myself and
my ability to help others. **1 2 3 4 5**

❏ I am a value provider. I am able
to get a fair, profitable price. **1 2 3 4 5**

❏ I am able to transfer my message. **1 2 3 4 5**

❏ I am authentic, ethical, honest, friendly,
believable, and trustworthy. **1 2 3 4 5**

❏ I respond in a nano-second. **1 2 3 4 5**

❏ I keep my promises. **1 2 3 4 5**

❏ I am persuasive, NOT pushy. **1 2 3 4 5**

❏ I am assertive, NOT aggressive. **1 2 3 4 5**

❏ I follow through (after the sale),
NOT just follow up. **1 2 3 4 5**

❏ I offer quality products, services,
and great service. **1 2 3 4 5**

❏ I am and we are easy to do business with. **1 2 3 4 5**

❐ I have an impeccable reputation – others
   are willing to speak for me.   **1 2 3 4 5**

❐ I am relationship driven, NOT quota driven,
   NOT transactional.   **1 2 3 4 5**

❐ I have and display character and
   confidence – I am resilient.   **1 2 3 4 5**

❐ My social footprint is connectable, viable,
   and valuable.   **1 2 3 4 5**

❐ I am personally responsible for my actions. **1 2 3 4 5**

❐ I am able to find and meet with
   the decision-maker.   **1 2 3 4 5**

❐ I am 100% reliable.   **1 2 3 4 5**

❐ I am trusted as a person and a provider.   **1 2 3 4 5**

❐ I have a 4x pipeline to sales goal.
   I never force an "end of the month" sale.   **1 2 3 4 5**

❐ I take actions to become referable.   **1 2 3 4 5**

❐ I am mission driven, NOT commission driven. **1 2 3 4 5**

How to Personalize the Test

There are 23 total key behavior statements. Go back and
review your answers. Check the boxes on the left where
you scored 1, 2, or 3. Those are your weak areas. The
checked boxes become your personalized game plan to
take better manifesto success actions. Now all you have to
do is take daily positive action on one or more of your self-
ratings. More helpful ideas, strategies and answers are on
the pages that follow.

Think twice before you speak, because your words and influence will plant the seed of either success or failure in the mind of another.

Napoleon Hill

The Rules of Before

Before you start, set your mind on YES

Before you present, prepare

Before you sell, believe

Before you add value, give value

Before you ask, give

Before you tell, ask

Before you answer, think

Before you push, pull

Before you brag, prove

Before you close, open

Before you take, give

Before you say "we," speak "you"

Jeffrey Gitomer

Manifesto
Principles

Principles before Policy.

Jeffrey Gitomer
KING of SALES

Hard work makes luck!

Mel Green
MENTOR

The "non-system" and "secret rules" of "not-selling."

Jeffrey, is there a system of selling?

No. But, there is a *non-system*.

Jeffrey, is there an easier way to sell than others?

Yes, but it requires hard work and dedication.

Jeffrey, this is getting complicated – is it easy or hard?

It's hard at first – then easy.

Jeffrey, come on man, give me the answers.

It's very advanced. It takes time to get to the results.

Jeffrey, I work hard, man. I'm ready for a better way.

This is unconventional, and flies in the face of "normal."

Jeffrey, I'm dying over here.

OK – But you're not gonna like this at first, because it's not the standard: Warm-up, probe, present, overcome objections, close, confirm, thank, leave. That's "how to make a sale." *People don't like to be sold – but they love to buy*™. This is a "non-system." It's the alternative to a bunch of manipulative tactics – it's a long-term winning strategy. This is how to make people want to buy.

This *non-system* is the most powerful, profitable, lucrative sales strategy ever developed – and it has very little to do with selling tactics. It has everything to do with creating an atmosphere where people want to buy. And just to be clear – this is not "how to sell" – this is how I sell.

And since I created the "non-system," I'm naming it after myself. The Gitomer "Non-System" of Selling.

Here are the 2.5 ground rules for applying the Gitomer "non-system."

1. It is learned and mastered over time. IT IS NOT A QUICK FIX. It won't help you make this month's quota, BUT it will help you achieve a lifetime of sales success, quotas included. I've been refining it for 25 years.

2. It assumes you believe in your company, your product, your service, and yourself. If those beliefs are not present, the rest of this information is a waste of your time. In sales if you *believe*, you have a chance to set an atmosphere to transfer that belief. And create an atmosphere where someone wants to BUY. Otherwise, it's a "sale" and you will fight "price." That would be a transaction. My "non-system" relies on *value*.

2.5 This non-system also assumes you are a student of sales and success and have a regular learning discipline. Oh, that. MAJOR CLUE: a regular learning discipline does not include re-runs of *Married with Children*, *Cheers,* or *ER*.

Trying to use a "system of selling" and it's not working, or at least not working well in all situations? All my sales life I've been deluged by "systems of selling." And all my sales life I've fought them as being bogus – or at the least manipulative.

No one system will work all the time – BUT specific elements of any system will always be applicable. I'm NOT saying don't learn systems – all sales knowledge is valuable. I am saying *be yourself in the sale, not the system*. With that in mind I created a "Non-System" of selling.

Not that systems are "wrong" – more that they don't always "fit" the situation. And that the salesperson focuses on the execution of the system to make the sale, rather than focusing on the prospect to make the sale.

Well, after all that build-up, this better be good. *Here are the 9.5 steps of how to make people want to buy, buy again, and tell others to buy:*

1. Become known by your prospects before you call on them. (hint: In sales it's not who you know. In sales it's who knows you.)

2. Give value first. (hint: Your brochure and literature may have value to you, but they have little or no value to the prospect.)

3. Create attraction – and be attractive. (hint: Make people want to know you by the business, market, and community actions you take.)

4. Get people (prospects) to call you, walk in your door, or ask for an initial meeting. (hint: Value attracts. No cold calling here.)

5. Make them like you, believe you, have confidence in you, and trust you. (hint: People buy from people they like and trust, but they gotta like you FIRST).

6. Make them perceive a difference between you and your competition. (hint: Make a list of what you're saying or doing you are CERTAIN is different from what your competition is saying or doing. Small list?)

7. Create an atmosphere where prospects want to buy. (hint: Ask compelling questions. Make your information seem or be valuable to them. Show prospects how they will use and benefit from your product or service, not what it does or how it works – and especially not how good you are.)

8. Ask them for the order. (hint: One of the biggest reasons prospects don't buy is that no one asks them to.)

9. Be so valuable and memorable that they come back for more – and tell someone else. (hint: What are your customers saying about you after a typical call, sale or transaction.)

9.5 Measure your success by the number of unsolicited referrals you get. (hint: It's the highest percentage sales lead in your arsenal.)

I'll make a deal with you – I'll provide more explanation, if you provide the hard work. Fair enough?...

INSTRUCTIONS FOR BEST RESULTS: Read the list of elements twice. Consider the entire big picture to gain understanding. In this "non-system," consider them as a whole, but master them individually. Here are the principles in detail. *The 9.5 steps of how to make people want to buy, buy again, and tell others to buy:*

1. Become known by your prospects before you call on them.

The big rule of selling is: *In sales it's not who you know. In sales it's who knows you.* To become known to your prospect, think of three ways that you can become a valuable part of their success. Your customer is looking for four things: sell their stuff, make a profit, keep their customers and employees loyal, and have no problems. Your job is to reach customers and prospects with information of value about those four subjects via e-mail, newsletter, other forms of publishing (like this book is to you), or through public speaking. To master this first and most important element is to become known as a "person of value" because you have provided your customer with information of value. Value Clue: Information about you and your product are considered of little or low value to your customer.

2. Give value first. Your brochure and literature may have value to you, but they have little or no value to the prospect. If you give valuable information to your customer before you give them your sales pitch, you have a decided advantage in being listened to. By giving value first, you earn the respect of your potential customer, so that he is as interested to hear about your product as he was to learn about the information that you provided him prior to your sales pitch. (See, I told you this wasn't going to be easy at first).

3. Create attraction – and be attractive. Make people want to know you because of the business, market, and community actions you take. The more value you provide, the more attractive you become. The more of a leadership role you decide to take, the more attractive you become. This has nothing to do with the clothing you wear or the car that you drive. Attraction is a state of being rather than a material circumstance.

4. Get people (prospects) to call you, walk in your door, or ask for an initial meeting. Value attracts. Cold calling repels. What information can you provide your customer that will compel them to call you for additional information? For example, when you send them your brochure, what about that brochure will make them call you for additional information? If the answer is nothing, then don't send the brochure. Send them three ways they can improve their profitability, and if they want the fourth one, call you on the phone or send you an email or fax you.

5. Make them like you, believe you, have confidence in you, and trust you. People buy from people they like and trust. Credibility is established with a combination of your self-belief and how believable your information is. Most salespeople make the mistake of giving a sales presentation. Who are you most likely to believe a car salesman or your next-door neighbor who owns the car? That same answer applies to your customers in your selling situations. Think about the people you do business with. Now think about the ones you've been doing business with for years. Because they know you and you know them, there is a comfort level in dealing with them. People who like you and trust you are your easiest and surest sale. Better stated, they want to BUY from you.

6. Make them perceive a difference between you and your competition. Make a list of what you're saying or doing you are CERTAIN is different from what your competition is saying or doing. Small list? Most prospects or customers perceive your product or service (copy machine, accounting service, website developer) to be pretty much like that of your competitors. Your single highest goal in a sales presentation is to create a *perceived difference*. I'd like to give you an answer on this one, but the answer lies in the reflection you see each morning when you look in your bathroom mirror. *You* are the difference, and your highest responsibility is to make your prospect perceive that difference. CLUE: The answer lies in your value, not your sales presentation.

7. Create an atmosphere where prospects want to buy. Ask compelling questions. Make your information valuable to them. Show prospects how they will use and benefit from your product or service, not what it does or how it works – and especially not how good you are. Ask yourself: *What makes you buy.* Isn't it a feeling you get that the risk is low and the value is high and the desire is great. Your customer or prospect is looking to buy (Gitomer's sales adage: *People don't like to be sold but they love to buy*™) and the best way to do this is for your sales presentation to take a new direction. A reverse direction. One where your customers, in the form of testimonials, speak for you instead of you speaking for yourself. That's a new direction.

8. Ask them for the order. One of the biggest reasons prospects don't buy is that no one asks them to. No matter what happens in any sales situation, your consciousness of purpose must be to ask for the order before you leave. It's the reason you walked in the door, other than providing valuable information, and helping the other person decide to buy. Asking for the order is not always manifest with a sales order. It may just be for the next step in the sales cycle that leads you to the order. In selling, you can never ask early enough, and you can never ask often enough for the commitment to buy.

9. Be so valuable and memorable that they come back for more – and tell someone else. What are your customers saying about you after a typical call, sale, or transaction? Is anyone picking up the phone and telling a story about how creative you were, how outstanding you were, or how incredible you were? If the answer is no, then you will lose out on the most valuable element of after-sale: word-of-mouth advertising that leads to an unsolicited referral.

9.5 Measure your success by the number of unsolicited referrals you get. It's the highest percentage sales lead in your arsenal. If you're looking for a sales report card, look no further than the number of people who call you on the phone wanting to buy. Because if ten people a day called you on the phone wanting to buy, you'd never have to sell again.

OK, there it is – The Gitomer "Non-System" of Selling. Master these elements and sales will be EASY. I promise – I've been doing it this way for years. With this "non-system" you can go out (or come in) to work and make almost every sale. I've just given you the secret formula to sell EVERYONE.

Most people won't do the hard work it takes to make sales easy.

Jeffrey Gitomer
KING of SALES

52.5

Principles of Manifesto Selling

Start with your core philosophy of sales …

Mine is five parts…
I give value first, I help other people,
I strive to be my BEST at what
I love to do, I establish long-term
relationships with everyone,
and I have fun… every day.

What's your philosophy?
Do you have one? Start writing it today!

AND… Know who the most
important person in the world is.

1. The two most important words in selling – you & why. The first thing the customer buys is you – the second thing they want to know is "why should I buy from you?"

2. Know "why you're selling" – know your own *why* first. Your "why" (your real reason for wanting success) builds your internal belief. When "why" is clear, everything is clear. Before you can affect and influence others, you must know yourself. To be the best you can be for others – first be the best you can be for yourself.

3. To get to your real why, it may be 4 or 5 "whys" deep, but if you get there you can sell (and find the hot button). Here's an example...

Why are you in sales? – I'm in sales to make more money.

Why? – I need more money to support my family.

Why? – Two of my kids start college in the next two years, and I want them to be able to choose a school based on quality not price.

Why? – My parents couldn't afford to send me to college.

Aha! Found my deep why. You can never get to greatness (manifesto greatness) until you find your *why?* and are willing to work for it.

4. The sale is in your head. The mindset by which you approach the sale will determine its outcome more than any other element of the selling process. The sale is in your head WAY BEFORE it's in your wallet.

5. Develop a five-part belief system that can't be penetrated.
Believe in your company. Believe in your product. Believe
in yourself. Believe you can differentiate FROM your
competition, and believe your customer is better off having
purchased from you.

6. Become valuable by giving value first. Make the prospect
perceive greater value in you and from you than quality
and service. I have practiced giving value and posting value
messages for more than 25 years. So far, it's working and my
phone is ringing.

7. Develop a selfish attitude about being the best. Unless you're
the best you can be for yourself, you'll never be the best you
can be to serve others. Don't cheer for athletes – cheer for
yourself. You deserve it.

8. Be your own Santa Claus. Provide your own gifts and
toys. Give yourself whatever you want. Most of us don't get
what we want for Christmas unless we tell someone what
we want – or if you're like me – go buy it yourself. For me,
every day is Christmas – know why? I deserve it.

**9. Know "what you sell" in terms of the customer – not in terms
of you.** People don't care what you do, unless they perceive
it helps them. The way you explain your business and
product determines the buying interest you create – say it in
terms of the prospect not you.

10. Sell it as if you were selling it to your own son or daughter.
Give advice with it, help learn it, and the advantages of
using it. Protect them.

11. Know your competitive advantage(s) – learn them from your customers. Here's how to define competitive advantage: Something that's extremely important to your customers at which you excel. (Competitive advantage has nothing to do with the competition.)

My competitive advantage is value and substance – make it yours.

12. People buy for their reasons not yours. Find out theirs first. Establishing their "why" is the basis of determining their true need(s).

13. Ask the wrong questions – get the wrong answers. The way you question will determine the way you sell. Refine yours every week, until their power is evident by the increase in your sales.

14. Develop and ask questions that make the prospect think about themselves and answer in terms of you. Make them evaluate new information. Get them to give you answers in the form of information about themselves, and in terms of your product or service.

15. Transition from a salesperson to a resource. Become valuable. The more value you bring to the table, the higher you'll be able to go in the organization.

16. Use the principle of leaning forward. Get the prospect to be interested in what you have to say.

Let the dog chase you.

17. Start your sale higher than you dare. The president of the company always knows how decisions are made and who makes them. Why begin the sale any lower?

18. Your ability to observe is as powerful as your ability to sell. Half the answers are there for you to see…if you're looking.

19. Get your phone to ring with qualified prospects by promoting. Advertising doesn't work – promotion does. Put yourself in a position to be seen, and become known as a person of value.

- I don't advertise first - I promote first. I don't sell first, I promote first.

- I get my phone to ring with qualified prospects – then I sell.

    EXAMPLE: I create articles and newsletters that feature customers so they can share with other prospects. I give talks and seminars at trade shows.

    NOTE: Exhibiting at trade shows is advertising. Speaking or giving a seminar at trade shows is promoting – it also proves leadership without saying "I'm a leader."

20. Your listening skills must be as good as your selling skills. Listening provides a wider path to the sale than talking. Listen with the intent to understand. Write down answers given by prospects.

21. Make the prospect prepare to see you. Get them to email you their needs, get the room ready, or bring in another decider. If the prospect is willing to prepare, it means they are interested.

22. Make your customers the heroes of your business. Fully explain the newsletter concept. Publicize others.

23. It may be your 10,000th time, but it's their first. Sell it with the same enthusiasm you had your first day on the job. Tell the prospect everything they need to know, not just what you think they need to know.

24. Customer types don't matter as much as customer characteristics and interests. If you spend 15 minutes trying to figure out what "type" he or she is, and I spend 15 minutes trying to find common ground and "the link," I will make the sale 74% more than you, and I don't care what "type" they were.

25. Know whose fault is it when the sale's not made. If they don't return your phone call, whose fault is that? If they decided to buy from the competition, whose fault is that? *Yours* – you couldn't get the prospect to lean forward. Don't *blame* yourself – take *responsibility* for it.

26. Do more than you're paid for. Become valuable. Become a resource for your company, your co-workers, and your customers. Invest in yourself and others will pay you dividends. Lifelong dividends.

27. Know your success formula by numbers – live it. Work backward.

28. Make up in numbers what you lack in skills (while you learn them). Fail your way to the top by synergizing numbers with lifelong learning.

Once you know how many no's it takes to get to yes – increase your no's.

29. Have the chutzpah to go past the line – to risk. Anyone know the dictionary definition of chutzpah? Chutzpah is loosely translated into English as gonads.

30. Sell for the relationship not the commission. If you make a sale you can earn a commission. If you make a friend, you can earn a fortune. In sales you don't make money – you earn it.

31. However you treat someone will come back to you tenfold. Don't do anyone bad or dirty under any circumstances. Follow Golden Rules one and two.

32. The little guy will become the big guy. Treat him that way from day one. All customers are equal.

33. Milk your own cows first. Maximize the business you already have, seek inside referrals. Network among customers to get to their peer friends.

34. One testimonial is worth one hundred sales pitches. It's real proof of who you are and what you do.

35. Testimonial letters can overcome objections one million times better than the best salesperson in the world. What better proof have you got? What better answer could you give?

Get the right testimonial, just walk in and say, "Here, read this!"

36. It's not a give and take situation – it's a give and give. What are you giving? How are you helping your customers grow?

Get them business to earn yours.

37. Use the principle of persistence/reluctance. Opposites attract. If they need you, you must persist until they buy you.

When would you go to the dentist if he didn't persist?

38. Call their sales department – for all the information in the world! Salespeople know EVERYTHING about EVERYONE and will gladly give info to a fellow salesperson.

39. Take advantage of technology, or lose to someone that did. Smartphone. Laptop. Tablet. Social Media. Blog. Podcast.

If your most important customer called you right now, how would you get the message and how long would it take you to return the call? Suppose they called your biggest competitor at the same time?

40. Be in front of people who can say yes 40% of your day. You don't need a time management course, you just need to buy a stopwatch. It's called stopwatch time management. Double your sales by being in front of decision-makers twice as much as you are now.

41. Plan for the next five years while others are asleep or numb. If you've been on the job for five years, you must be thinking five years from now – you must plan for that and sell accordingly. Synergize long-term plans with short-term quotas and "having a good month."

If you plan it right (and promote right), soon all months will be "GREAT."

Get up before everyone else. Plan while others watch the news.

Change and adjust your plan every 30 days.

42. If the rules you have to work by don't work for you – work someplace else. Or find a way to follow the rules without it affecting your attitude and turn you into a puker.

43. Ask for an opinion often. From people you respect (who have no axe to grind). And from the person you're trying to sell. Not only does it give you the prospect's perspective (the only one that matters), but it's a great test close.

44. Better physical fitness leads to better mental fitness. Leads to more sales. Lighten your load. Work out daily. Eat less crap. Drink water.

45. In anything you have to say…less is more.

46. Your ability to recognize opportunity will set you apart from the others. Opportunity often shows up in the form of adversity.

47. Your attitude will allow you to see opportunity. Or not. And determine if you are able to capitalize on it.

48. If you take "no" seven times, it will lead you to YES!

49. More salespeople fail from complacency than from inadequacy. The better you get at sales, the more you must rededicate yourself to being (and getting) better. The more successful you become, the more you must study success and rededicate yourself to being a greater success. Or you will lose what you've got to someone hungrier than you. A tortoise. It's not what you say – it's what you do. Boy, if we could just make that a law for politicians.

50. You deserve it. Never sell yourself short. Get what makes you feel GREAT. You are the greatest if you think you are.

51. Use the force. The subconscious mind will always carry you through – if you believe it will. Hey, it worked in Star Wars didn't it? I rest my point.

52. To develop the MANIFESTO Slight Edge, follow ALL the principles with these easy to understand and implement axioms....

- Know and live by the mantra of… **Take responsibility. Stop blaming.**
- Simple self-disciplines repeated over time will lead to success.
- Wake up to the 5 disciplines: Read. Write. Prepare. Think. Create
- Small errors in judgment repeated over time will lead to failure.
- One cigarette. One drink. One TV show. One blame.

52.5 You don't get great at selling in a day. *You get great at selling day by day.* What did you do great today?

Salespeople already
know everything…
Problem is, they just don't do it.
"Doing it" puts you ahead of the people
that only "know it."

Jeffrey Gitomer
KING of SALES

People buy for their reasons…
not yours.
Find their reasons first,
and they're more likely to BUY.

(Note: Control the conversation and
get their reasons by asking.)

Don't "QUALIFY" anyone. Just "LIKE" them.

Jeffrey Gitomer
KING of SALES

Mastering Manifesto Social Selling

Elements and ideas to employ so you can create the "National Agenda."

- Attract, engage, connect, sell & deliver – social selling allows you to do this and more.

- Networking is social – LinkedIn and Facebook – you're already doing it personally, do it for business.

- Attract followers with value messaging and maintain followers with value messaging.

- Facebook, YouTube, and Instagram offers some form of live broadcast. Live is the new black.

- Podcast is blacker than live.

- Target audiences with well-placed, inexpensive ads.

Minimum numbers for social success

1,000 Facebook likes

500 Twitter followers

501 LinkedIn connections

25 YouTube Videos

Email value messages

Weekly Podcast

Attract – Engage – Connect – Sell – Keep

*The Internet is the world's most fertile selling ground.
Plant seeds of VALUE, and reap attraction,
reputation, sales, and loyalty.
Social is no longer an option – it's an IMPERATIVE.*

SOCIAL SELLING DEFINED – Your ability to attract and convince others that you are the best choice.

SOCIAL PLATFORM – You MUST be active on all formats. You MUST post something consistently to each media.

VALUE POST – The key words in posting are VALUE TO THE READER.

ONLINE AND OFF-LINE REPUTATION – Your post and other's posts about you create lifetime reputation.

THE IMPERATIVE OF SOCIAL PROOF – Testimonials are the foundation of sales and reputation.

VIDEO PROOF – Video is better than text. Enough said.

ONLINE UNSOLICITED REFERRALS – Value out brings calls in.

Go to my website for my free **RETWEETABLES EBOOK** – copy this link in your browser buygitomer.com/products/retweetables

Your customer wants to do business with a somebody not a nobody.

Jeffrey Gitomer
KING of SALES

12.5 skills every MANIFESTO salesperson must master

1. The consistency of your YES! Attitude

2. The depth of your belief

3. A firm understanding of providing value
   a. different from, rather than compare to
   b. perceived value – NOT added value

4. Your ability to attract, engage, and connect socially and face-to-face

5. Your social platform, reputation, and Google-ability

6. The ability to ask an emotional question

7. The dynamics of your presentation skills

8. Your ability to transfer a message

9. Giving service that comes from your heart

10. The most effective strategies for earning (closing) sales

11. A genuine desire to build a friendship and relationship

12. Knowing the difference between blame and responsibility

12.5 The difference between telling, asking, and earning

THE SUBTLE SECRET: Focusing on help, not sale.

Manifesto Strategies

The best way to get loyalty
is to give loyalty.

The best way to get a referral
is to give a referral.

The best way to get trust
is to give trust.

Jeffrey Gitomer
KING of SALES

If you're not a half an hour early,
you're late!

Earl Pertnoy
MENTOR

Are you outstanding in *your* field or out standing in *a* field?

You can be "in the field" or you can "lead the field."

Which do you think is better? Lead the field, of course. Which are you? Uh oh. In the field.

And some of you are saying, "Oh, Jeffrey I couldn't lead my field. I'm just a sales rep." And you are wrong.

Most leaders start at the bottom. Every great chess player was once a beginner. Great ball players started in T-ball, Little League, and Pop Warner. You included.

How do you make the transition? Not a simple answer – but well worth it to explore. And there's some great news – you don't have to be the biggest to be the leader. You don't even have to be the best to be the leader. You only have to be *perceived* as a leader by your customers and other peers.

And you don't have to lead the world – you just need to establish a *leadership position.* **You just need to be** *perceived* **as being one notch ahead of your competition. That seems a bit more doable, now, doesn't it?**

And then there's the question, "why should I be, or why do I need to be a leader?" Money answer – leaders have an easier time attracting business, and are called upon when answers are needed. Power answer: They are a resource for information and influence.

Everyone in the field knows the leader – not everyone in the field knows the salesman – and in sales there is a little-known truth that can make all the difference in your success: As previously stated: **In sales it's not who you know – in sales it's who knows you.**

Here are 11.5 elements to help you become a leader in your field:

1. **Read about your field from old sources.** Know the history of your field and the people who influenced it. You must study this for 15 minutes a day.

2. **Know what's new, now.** Know your present situation and position.

3. **Know what's next.** Stay on the cutting edge of your market's information. This means networking in high places, and having the right contacts.

4. **Follow the "experts" and see if you can best them.** When you see what others have done, figure out how to improve (not criticize) it.

5. **Write about it.** Writing forces you to be a trendsetter, and you are seen as a (well positioned) leader.

6. **Speak in public.** Develop one area of expertise and get in front of a group of influencers and impress them.

7. **Study creativity.** A science that will be mandatory to master in the 21st century – creativity may be the only thing that separates you from the ordinary – and the others.

8. **Befriend the influential people.** Become known as a person of value, and you will find it easy to make friends in high places.

9. **Have one or two big people or customers who love you.** You need supportive fans that cheer about you behind your back, and give you a boost.

10. **Give value first.** This element could be at the top of the list. Become known as a person who gives more than takes.

11. **Study the science of positioning.** Create ways for you to become known. Improve ways to stay in front of your customers and your market.

11.5 **Find a mentor and earn your way in. You want to be a leader? Learn from other leaders.**

These elements must be mastered one at a time. You don't become a leader in a day – you become a leader day by day.

Oh yeah, two more minor things – You gotta believe you can – and you gotta be passionate about what you're trying to achieve.

Whew! Tall order – but that's why there are so few leaders. It's hard work. In my study of sales success I have been startled most by this revelation: Most salespeople won't do the (up front) hard work that it takes to make selling easy. When you arrive in the leadership position – making sales is easier – and more fun.

I just finished listening to the first recordings of Earl Nightingale's famous series, *"Lead the Field."* It was originally published on 33 1/3 speed records back in the 60's. Earl Nightingale was one of my mentors and he never knew it. His records and tapes made me understand that I could accomplish anything if I believed strongly and worked hard. His message is as timely and true today as it was then.

Here are a few Earl Nightingale quotes to fuel your ambition to dominate!

1. **Success is the progressive realization of a worthy goal or ideal.**

2. **People with goals succeed because they know where they're going.**

3. **Whatever we plant in our subconscious mind and nourish with repetition and emotion will one day become a reality.**

4. **All you need is the plan, the roadmap, and the courage to press on to your destination.**

5. **The more intensely we feel about an idea or a goal, the more assuredly the idea, buried deep in our subconscious, will direct us along the path to its fulfillment.**

6. Picture yourself in your mind's eye as having already achieved this goal. See yourself doing the things you'll be doing when you've reached your goal.

7. There is a time when one must decide either to risk everything to fulfill one's dreams or sit for the rest of one's life in the backyard.

8. People are where they are because that is exactly where they really want to be—whether they will admit that or not.

9. We all walk in the dark and each of us must learn to turn on his or her own light.

10. The opposite of courage in our society is not cowardice... it is conformity.

11. Don't concern yourself with the money. Be of service … build … work … dream … create! Do this and you'll find there is no limit to the prosperity and abundance that will come to you.

12. Get into a line that you will find to be a deep personal interest, something you really enjoy spending twelve to fifteen hours a day working at, and the rest of the time thinking about.

13. A great attitude does much more than turn on the lights in our worlds; it seems to magically connect us to all sorts of serendipitous opportunities that were somehow absent before the change.

14. Work never killed anyone. It's worry that does the damage. And the worry would disappear if we'd just settle down and do the work.

15. We can let circumstances rule us, or we can take charge and rule our lives from within.

15.5 You become what you think about all day long (the strangest secret in the world).

Manifesto Challenge

What are you doing to lead your field?

The answer is usually two words:
not enough.

ARE YOU MANIFESTO READY?

Take the online self-assessment and see:
www.gitomer.com/manifesto
It's private, it's free,
and it shows you where you are
vs. where you need to be to dominate.

On March 2, 1962, an unbreakable basketball record was set.

I'm a Wilt Chamberlain fan. I have been since the late 1950s.

Chamberlain grew up in Philadelphia. (I grew up in Philadelphia's suburbs.) He went to Overbrook High School and then decided to go the University of Kansas.

He dropped out of college after two seasons, and because in those days you could not enter professional basketball until after your senior class had graduated, he played one and half years with the Harlem Globetrotters.

In the summer of 1960, while I was attending Pine Forest (a summer camp), Wilt came as a Harlem Globetrotter. (He had previously been a kitchen boy at the camp.) He put on a brief exhibition and signed autographs. I was 14. I had the presence of mind to ask Wilt for his autograph on a postcard. At camp we were required to write home every day.

The postcard I sent home that day read: ***Dear Mom and Dad, I played ball with Wilt the Stilt today. Here's his autograph. Please save this postcard. Love, Jeff***

My mother, rest her soul, saved the postcard for 25 years. I found it with all the other postcards and letters she had saved as I was going through her personal artifacts after she passed away. That was a moment all by itself.

I don't know the value of a 1960 Wilt Chamberlain authentic autograph, but I do know that if someone offered me $100,000, I would pass. Some things have no price in spite of the clichés you may have heard.

Back to Wilt.

You can argue the fact that Wilt was the best basketball player of all time. Many will agree. Many will disagree. I don't really care about the people who disagree.

WILT CHAMBERLAIN SET THE STANDARD

Wilt Chamberlain's records are still on the books. He was the only NBA player to score 4,000 points in a season. He set NBA single-game records for most points (100), most consecutive field goals (18), and most rebounds (55). His most mind-boggling stat was the 50.4 points per game he averaged during the 1961-62 season. He also averaged 48.5 minutes of play per game that same year (that's every minute, of every game, plus overtime).

Wilt entered the NBA as a Philadelphia Warrior (based on the territorial draft system that was in place at that time), briefly went to San Francisco when the Warriors went there, then rejoined Philadelphia as a 76er, and ended his career in Los Angeles as a Laker.

When Wilt retired...

- He was the all-time leader in career points with 31,419. (Later passed by Kareem Abdul-Jabbar, Karl Malone, and Michael Jordan.)

- He held the record for most rebounds with 23,924. (Will never be passed.)

- He led the NBA in scoring for seven years in a row. Most games with 50+ points: 118. Most consecutive games with 40+ points: 14. Most consecutive games with 30+ points: 65. Most consecutive games with 20+ points: 126. Highest rookie scoring average: 37.6 per game. Highest field goal percentage in a season: .727. (And with many of these records, the player in second place is far, far behind.)

- HOLY CRAP!

INTERESTING FACT ABOUT WILT: He never fouled out of a basketball game during the entire length of his career, yet he also led the league in blocked shots and rebounds.

THE RECORD: On March 2, 1962, while playing against the New York Knicks, in Hershey, Pennsylvania, in front of about 4,500 people, Wilt scored 100 points. It's a record that will never be broken.

The game was not televised. I listened to it on the radio.

The reason I'm writing this is that Wilt Chamberlain did not just set records, **he set standards.** His athletic prowess was so great that he changed the rules of the game.

Wilt was so massive and such a great rebounder that they widened the foul lanes to prevent Wilt from complete basketball domination. He was a game changer AND a rule changer.

- **What are you able to change about your career or process?**

- **What level are you playing at? Top, middle, or below average?**

- **What records are you setting that will last 50 years?**

- **What contributions have you made?**

Wilt Chamberlain was colorful and controversial.
Wilt spoke his mind.
Wilt coached and mentored MANY other players to success.
You either loved him or hated him.
I loved him.

Most people don't realize that Wilt wasn't just a basketball player, he was a world-class athlete. He set a state high school record in high jump, and after he retired from professional basketball, he won the two-man volleyball championship more than once.

Please don't confuse this as just a tribute to the late, great Wilt Chamberlain. Rather, it's a commentary on setting standards, breaking records, and the ability to have so much skill that the rules are changed to level the playing field. That's what Wilt Chamberlain was to basketball.

Wilt set the standard.
What standards have you set?
What standards could you set?

Free Git⅄Bit...If you'd like to see some amazing images of Wilt, including a copy of the postcard I sent to my parents back in 1960, go to www.gitomer.com and enter the word WILT in the GitBit box.

Good to Great.
Are you "good" or maybe slightly below?

Jim Collins immortal business bestseller, *Good to Great*, created a revolution in many businesses and an explosion in book sales. The book was adopted, adapted, taught, and implemented. In many instances, companies did go from good to great – or at least from good to very good.

The key is these companies sought improvement. Self-improvement. Whether it was from within, or from an outside group of impartial experts, the concept was and is to "get better." Great is an elusive target. Collins knew it.

The concept is not complicated. It revolves around self-assessment, an agreed-upon game plan of action, measurable results, and an overall spirit that includes individual work, teamwork, and remarkable leadership. So far it's simple.

The real issue is, and the thing that has always bothered me about the book, is that the beginning premise assumes you are "good." Most companies and their people are not. Most businesses are not. And you see them every day, going out of business.

Many companies try to maximize profit by cutting costs, or worse, cutting quality, or way worse, cutting service offerings. Then customers get angry and tell other potential customers through social media, or some form of online reporting like TripAdvisor or Angie's List. Then reputation is somewhere between questionable and lost. Followed by a downturn in business.

In 1996, I wrote this customer service truth: "It never costs as much to fix the problem as it does to not fix the problem." Decades later, that statement has never been more true.

Good to Great was published in 2001 way before social media dominated the scene. Companies no longer have to self-assess; all they have to do is go to their Facebook page where their customers have already done it. And there's usually a huge gap between what companies and their leadership THINK they are, and what their customers SAY they are. I will always take the latter as the true picture.

So the real challenge is not how you get from good to great. It's how you get from crappy to good. Things like rundown hotels, lousy food in a restaurant, rude clerk in a retail store, long lines to be served, long waits on hold, not keeping up with technology, and poor management seem to be pervasive in our society.

An easy way to begin your march up the ladder to greatness (or even just goodness) is to talk to more of your customers. Get their views both online and in person. Get video from them if you can. Create a YouTube channel that features their voices.

"Voice of customer" in any format forms a clear picture of exactly where you are in their opinion, what they like, what they expect, and what they wish was better. It creates a solid foundation from which to start. What better place to start than from the customer's perspective of what would help you get better?

Oh, it's also your reputation. And it's also FREE!

This same lesson applies to salespeople. How "good" are you? Is "good" your starting point? If you didn't make your sales goals last year, can you honestly say you're good? Or would you fall just below good? Somewhere between crappy and good?

Keep in mind that as I'm attempting to help salespeople assess themselves, they are the lifeblood, and the cash flow, and the profit of the business. Businesses that don't make enough sales go out of business. Were they good businesses gone bad? Were they good businesses with bad salespeople? Or were they bad businesses that failed? I'll take the latter.

And while I realize that I'm taking a superficial view, not going into detail about quality of leadership, quality of service, quality of product, employee retention, or customer retention, I maintain my premise that "voice of customer," both internal and external, will net better truth and a better foundation than a bunch of leaders and consultants sitting around a table coming up with ideas. Many of them self-serving.

Back to salespeople for a moment… There is no quick fix to get a salesperson from good to great, or from below good to above good. But there is a real answer: *training*. Repetitive training until the salesperson goes from understanding and willingness to application, to proficiency, and finally mastery through daily action.

Be willing to measure your results. CAUTION: Measurement isn't how many cold calls you made this week. Weak measurement. Don't measure failure, measure success. Measure pipeline dollars. Measure sale to profit percentage. Measure new customers secured. Measure reorders.

Make measurement a learning experience, not a punishment.

Good to Great isn't just a book and a concept; it's also a challenge. The ultimate desired outcome, wherever you enter the process is: IMPROVEMENT. Where are YOU on that path? How big is the "room for improvement" in your world?

Most salespeople are GOOD, very few are GREAT.

What's the difference? I have added a "good" list and a "great" list. You won't like them. Great is rare. It requires years of hard work and a dedication to excellence. Good news for great seekers: Hard work is a rare currency that easily converts to cash.

You don't get great at sales in a day – You get great at sales day by day.

Jeffrey Gitomer
KING of SALES

Good is:

- Making quota

- Giving proposals and bids

- Closing 10-20% of sales

- Keeping your CRM current

- Having a mediocre social presence

- Having a mediocre Google presence

- "Closing" sales

- Begging for appointments

- Trouble getting to final decision-maker

Great is:

- Belief in yourself and your ability

- Total preparation in terms of the customer and how they win

- Dedication to lifelong learning

- Allocation of time for maximum productivity

- Social presence and relevance – website, on all relevant platforms

- The ability to differentiate FROM

- The ability to uncover the real motive to buy

- **The ability to transfer a message**

- **The ability to prove value**

- **The ability to incorporate the "voice of customer" proof factor**

- **The ability to build relationships**

- **The ability to understand and earn loyalty**

- **The ability to earn referrals**

- **Winning on value not price or bid**

- **Having a GREAT Google reputation**

Realities:

- **Responsibility vs. Blame**

- **Converting no into know**

- **Learning from a final no**

- **Knowing the difference between sales plan, sales quota, and sales dominance**

Manifesto Moment

CATCH: There's always a catch to a "sure thing." All you have to add is hard work. Damn hard work. Here's the secret rule of sales success that goes with the above elements: *Most salespeople won't do the hard work it takes to make selling easy.*

Jeffrey Gitomer

A goal is a dream with a plan. And other fairy tales.

My mother never went to Europe.

She talked about it, dreamed about it – even opened a travel agency at age 55. Never got there. She died 15 years later, never achieving the goal. Oh, she achieved plenty of other goals. But not that one.

I went to Europe for the first time at age 20. One of the things I wanted to do there was study French. It's a beautiful language. Romantic, expressive, cultural. Never did. Tried, never did. I've been to Europe 30 times, France 20 times. Never learned the language. Oh, I know a few hundred words, but can't converse or understand conversation.

Unmet goals.

Got unmet goals?

Personal goals start as thoughts and dreams. Business goals may have those attributes, but often business goals are handed to you by a superior. Sales goals, sales plans, sales numbers, pipelines, funnels, and various benchmarks for you to achieve for THEM.

You then make a goal to achieve their goal. And many salespeople do. But many (most) do not. Management will refer to those who did not meet their goal as "weak." That way they don't have to take any blame or responsibility for their "weak" people.

Meantime, you have your goals. Whatever they are – visit Europe, speak French, go on a vacation, buy a house, get a new car, take off weight, stop smoking, get married, get divorced, have a child, get your child out of the house – you have your own PERSONAL goals.

In the shower this morning, I came up with a thought as to WHY goals are met and unmet. Achieved and not achieved. It centers around the old definition about goals that has always bugged me: "A goal is a dream with a plan."

That statement is not only wrong, it's dangerous. It tells you you'll never achieve your goals unless you make a plan. I don't get it. I make very few plans, and I achieve tons of goals.

There are lots of goals that are not "dreams." Did you dream your sales quota? No, you were sent an email or given a sheet of paper. No dream there. My first trip to Europe was never a dream. It was an opportunity that popped up, and I took advantage of it. No dream, no plan – just an airplane ticket, a passport, and some money.

Here are the elements that I believe define and comprise the dream, goal, and achievement process:

Thinking. Ideas pop into your head. Write them down.

Dreaming and daydreaming. Thoughts make (let) your mind wander to desire, possibility, and "what if." I love to daydream. Don't confuse daydreams with pipedreams. You will never win the lottery.

Observing. Looking closely at the world and your world to see what it is that you really want to be, do, and have.

Opportunity. Recognizing it. Seizing it. And taking advantage of it.

Risk tolerance determines outcomes. If you perceive the goal is too "risky," you'll pass. If you wanna achieve, you gotta risk.

Coulda, woulda, shoulda. The words of people unwilling to risk. "I coulda been a contender, I coulda had class and been somebody." Marlon Brando, in his role as Terry Mallon playing in *On The Waterfront* – 1954.

Desire. Your level of desire will determine the length of time to achievement.

Want. Want it bad? Like desire, your level of "want" will determine the length of time to achievement.

Need. Need is a stronger circumstance than desire or want. Your need-reality will generate your level of achievement action.

Intention. Intentions PRECEDE actions. If you don't intend to, you won't achieve, even if you want to. What are your intentions?

Dedication. If it's a business goal, you have to dedicate the time to study and prepare. If it's a personal goal, you have to dedicate small amounts of time to steadily achieve.

Persistence. The sister of dedication, it's the stick-to-itiveness that pushes you to achievement.

Action for the day or the moment. Plans change, actions are in the NOW. Take some. An apple a day.

Skill set. Maybe your skills are precluding you from achievement. Maybe you need to study, practice, or enlist the aid of others.

Love of what you do, or what it is. Love breeds passion. Passion breeds action. Action breeds achievement.

For who? Why? If you have a motive, it may provide additional motivation. Don't be a martyr. Do it for yourself first. Understanding "for who" and "why" will help you achieve as much as any other aspect of this process.

Self-belief in every aspect of the process. You must believe in yourself BEFORE you can believe in the achievement of your goals. Think you can.

Mission. If your goal is different from your mission, it will lack the passion to become a reality.

Visibility. Post it where you can see it. Keep your goals top-of-mind – top-of-mind's-eye. I have my goals on my bathroom mirror. Do you?

2013

2018

Support and encouragement. When others are cheering you on, and encouraging you to achieve, it's a mental miracle.

Serendipity. I have defined it before as, "God's way of remaining anonymous." But it's more than that. Serendipity is that moment when chance and opportunity collide. And it's at that moment when you are challenged to grasp it, and make yourself and your loved ones better off. Successful. Fulfilled. You reached for the brass ring, and you caught hold.

NOTE WELL: If you get what you want, you better be ready. Ready to capitalize, ready to grow, ready to take advantage of, ready to share, and ready to enjoy – but not overindulge.

Brief background:

My philosophy of success incorporates my knowledge of business, sales, and personal development history.

I believe that if you don't know how things happened, then you will not understand why things are happening, where things are right now, and you will not be able to create or find a great game plan for the future.

Easy for me to say, I've written 15 books, and established my legacy as the King of Sales. And not too shabby at personal development, attitude, social media, and social selling either.

But please also note, I worked my ass off as an outlier while you were watching TV or at a party. I put in my 10,000+ hours in writing, speaking, and selling – and at this point in my life and career, helping you succeed.

That's the mission – HELP YOU SUCCEED – you have to decide how to accept it, and what to do about it.

Just for fun, take a look at a few videos of what happens just after I step out of the shower… www.youtube.com/buygitomer – search "on reflection"

The 95/95 Proposition. Which 95 Are You?

When a prospective customer calls you on the phone, and for some reason or another wants to buy – either they heard something good about you, or they read something about you, or they read something you wrote, or they watched something of yours, or someone referred them to you – the odds are close to 95% in your favor that you can make a sale and build a relationship.

Not bad odds.

REASON: The prospective customer called you, seeking information in the hope of making a purchase.

BACK TO REALITY: You come into your office and you sit at your desk. Today's the day you're going to (have to) make 100 phone calls (cold calls) to prospective customers. The odds are 95% of them will end up somewhere between "no" and hang up. Bad odds. And, of the other 5% that displayed some form of interest, one may eventually end up buying.

The problem is you will have to go through every sales gyration and your entire sales cycle to make that happen. Product offering, appointment, proposals, biddings, follow-up ad nauseam, finding the right decision-maker, and other walls of selling that you have erected based on your (or your company's) inability to be a marketplace value provider.

RECAP: You will make the sale 95% of the time when you RECEIVE an unsolicited call from a prospective customer. You will lose the sale 95% of the time when you MAKE an unsolicited call to a prospective customer.

YESTERDAY: For the past ten years (yesterday), it's likely that you or your business have been winning sales by capturing low-hanging fruit and you, as a salesperson, have thought to yourself, "I'm pretty good. I made president's club."

TODAY: All of a sudden you get to today, and you're looking around for fruit. It's nowhere to be found. And now you're in scramble mode for several reasons:

1. **You've built no social media platform.**

2. **You have no video testimonials to prove your value or the value of purchasing your product.**

3. **You have built little or no reputation in your marketplace.**

4. **Your product or your service is highly competitive, and it's difficult for you to differentiate yourself from the people you hate. Your competition. Worse: Amazon.com.**

4.5 **You have no value message that you send to your existing customers week after week.**

If you even have marketing messages or sales messages, they PUSH rather than PULL. They repel rather than attract.

TOMORROW: Which brings me to tomorrow. Or as they say at Disneyland, "Tomorrowland." You believe in your heart when the present economic situation changes, in "Tomorrowland" it will be way, way better, and everything will be just fine – and, of course, you will live happily ever after, making president's club again.

You might want to take that strategy next door to "Fantasyland" and shake hands with Mickey, Minnie, and especially Goofy.

There's an old expression that says, "If you want things to get better, you have to get better." If you haven't prepared for this time, or tomorrow, then NOW is the time to dig in. Stronger, faster, harder, and with more determination than ever.

When sales are tough, your competitors will be coming at your existing customers with offers that appeal to their pocketbook.

- **You have to provide valuable service,**

- **You have to be a value partner, and**

- **You have to be a value provider.**

If not, you'll either lose the account, or worse, be asked to match the price. (In the land of profit, matching a price is the same as losing.)

Now is the time to invest in yourself. And now is the time to invest in your customers in order to get the 95% pendulum to swing in your direction. Now is the time for value.

There are very few alternatives to what I'm recommending – and of those alternatives none are as valid as what I'm suggesting. Many salespeople at this moment are somewhere between whiny and panicky. They're worried about their jobs when they should be worried about their customer's well-being. They're worrying about the state of the world when they should be concentrating on the state of their customer's loyalty.

The 95% success strategy is very simple, but it requires WORK if you want to be on the receiving end of an unsolicited call:

- **Become a consistent value provider, especially to existing customers.**

- **Use your social media platform to broadcast value messages that existing and potential customers can benefit from.**

- **Build your reputation impeccably.**

- **Get your existing customers to endorse you, support you, and stay loyal to you.**

- **Utilize the strategy employed by every great athlete: self-talk equals self-performance.**

Tell yourself you're going to get the ball over the plate.
Tell yourself you're going to hit a home run.
Tell yourself you're going to return the punt for a touchdown.
And picture yourself doing it.

Figure out where your value message is with respect to your customer's perception of it, and their willingness to receive it.

Then do the one thing that 95% of salespeople will not do:

Work your ass off. Today.

Jeffrey Gitomer
KING of SALES

Here are a few strategies to get your phone to ring with prospective customers:

Your weekly value message: Subscribe to my weekly value message *Sales Caffeine* today. Read it for help, and use it as a model of a value-driven weekly message. Create yours. The more value you provide, the more your phone will ring.

Your podcast: Have you listened to our SELL or DIE podcast? Thousands of people do. Podcasts are a great way to show and provide value. Why not do yours on Facebook Live and repost it afterwards?

Your website: Have you registered yourname.com? Probably not. A one-page website with your philosophy of how you treat customers will get hits and a more important factor...

Your Google factor: Ever Google yourself? What comes up? For most salespeople it's either nothing or not enough. Your messages, your podcast, and your website will make you rise to the top of page one.

Wanna raise your percentage of sales success? Change your prospect.

Where are you on the percentage scale of sales?

How many out of ten can you close?

Well, Mr. Sales-big-shot, forget your percentage. It ain't all that good anyway. If you want to raise it by 50% – you heard me, FIFTY percent, just change the TYPE of sale you're making.

Huh?

The type of sale you make has more to do with why you're making it, and who you're making it with, than your fancy, manipulative, pushy closing techniques.

The old sales adage goes, all things being equal, people want to do business with their friends. *All things being not quite so equal, people STILL want to do business with their friends.*

Well, let's look behind that adage.

What are the "types" of sales calls you can make? I've listed them and given some insight as to why. Now I'm giving you the insight and the reality.

THE Lowest percentage: **Cold call.** Face it, the cold call is diminishing. Voicemail and security have taken away all the fun. Successful penetration is sporadic and there are MUCH better avenues of approach. PLUS, cold calling pisses people off.

Low percentage: **Appointed sales call from a cold call.** If you are lucky (or good) enough to have made an appointment someplace, this is OK, but still a low percentage based on the lack of qualification as to need. ***Hard work needed:*** There's no real formula for cold call success, but you can be smart about it – calling at the right times, a bit of pre-call research, and a ton of personal preparation in both sales training and category selection.

Fair percentage: **A response from an ad or direct mail or unsolicited email campaign.** Better than a cold call, but not by much. Most of these inquiries are about "how much?"

Semi-good percentage: **Appointed sales call from a networking event or trade show.** At least there has been some contact. You have a name, a card, and a person somewhat willing to take your call and make an appointment. ***Hard work needed:*** A networking plan and a 30-second personal commercial to qualify the prospect faster. Then there is the networking itself. Invest the time and work the plan. It will pay HUGE financial and personal dividends.

Pretty good percentage: **A social media inquiry.** A report card on your presence, or lack thereof. These people are saying, "I follow you, and like what you have to say, and want to know more." This is the new cold call, you just haven't figured it out yet.

Pretty good percentage: **A web inquiry.** Someone asking for more info from your website either on a web-call or a direct call is also a report card. It says your site is both interesting and navigable.

Pretty good percentage: **An email blast to your existing customers.** These are people who have already purchased. You have already established value and built confidence – maybe even some trust.

Good percentage: **Proactive call from a prospect.** Knows of you, interested, and wants more help. Can you convert?

Real good percentage: **A referral from another customer.** Should be a sale every time.

Real good percentage: **An unsolicited referral.** Hard work needed to get them: easy to convert once they call.

Highest percentage: **Sale or reorder from a present customer.** They know you, like you, trust you, believe in you, and have confidence you'll deliver. ***Hard work needed:*** Service between the sale. Stay in front of with value. Develop a relationship. Build trust through performance. Help them build their business. REALITY: None of this occurs making a cold call and running to the next.

AUTHOR'S NOTE: I know I'm going to get a bunch of emails telling me how great you are at cold calling and how cold calling works and how much money you made cold calling. Great – that was ten years ago. Wake up and smell the internet.

The Worst Way

The key to success at the cold call is *building a belief system*. Belief in yourself, your company, and what you sell. The more belief you have – better stated – *the more you believe that what you sell will help others,* the easier time you will have making cold calls. Here are the 4.5 basic beliefs you must own before you can start the cold call process:

1. I believe my company is the best.

2. I believe my products or services are the best.

3. I believe I am the best.

4. I believe I can differentiate myself from the competition, NOT compare myself to them.

4.5 I believe that when my customer buys, they will be better off having purchased from me.

Cold calling will test these beliefs right away. Especially when you begin to get rejected. Look at the real benefit of the cold call – Since all salespeople seek to improve their selling skills, the cold call presents a great opportunity to learn to sell.

REALITY: Cold calling is a lousy opportunity to make a sale. By the percentages, the lowest. By degree of difficulty, the hardest. By the intelligent ways to sell, the dumbest.

Pushy, aggressive, obnoxious, assertive, or professional. Which are you?

Sales reps get a bad rap for trying to sell too hard.

You've heard the term "pushy salesman" or "aggressive salesperson" or even "obnoxious salesman." How do those phrases make you feel?

And salespeople go to great lengths NOT to be perceived as pushy or aggressive or obnoxious – so they (maybe you) go to the opposite end of the spectrum and try to be, or be known as, professional.

BEWARE and BE AWARE: A professional sales call is okay, but boring. Professional meetings typically have no outcome. Or worse, they result in never-ending follow-up, void of sales. Not good. Here's a good way to think about professionalism: your customer must *perceive* you as a professional person. It's more of a look on your part, and a perception on the part of the customer. In today's world of selling, professionalism is a given. Your words, actions, and deeds take over from there.

Professionalism is not bad, but professionalism alone will not net sales.

MAJOR AHA! Between pushy, aggressive, obnoxious, and professional lies a middle ground – a ground where sales are made. It's known as *assertive.*

CAUTION: Assertiveness is not a word – it's a strategy and a style. It's not just "a way in which you conduct yourself." Rather, it's a full-blown strategy that has elements to master way before assertiveness can begin and be accepted as a style of selling.

BEWARE and BE AWARE: Assertiveness is a GOOD style of selling as long as you understand, and have mastered, the elements that make "assertive" acceptable on the part of the customer.

WHERE DOES ASSERTIVENESS COME FROM?

- **The root of assertiveness is belief.** Your belief in what you do, your belief in who you represent, your belief in the products and services that you sell, your belief in yourself, your belief that you can differentiate yourself from your competitor (not compare yourself to), and your *firm* belief that the customer is better off having purchased from you. These are not things you believe in your head. Rather, these are things you must believe in your heart. Deep belief is the first step in creating an assertive process. Until you believe, mediocrity is the norm. Once you believe in your heart, all else is possible.

- **An Attitude of Positive Anticipation.** In order to be assertive, positive attitude or *YES! Attitude* is not enough. You must possess an "Attitude of Positive Anticipation." This means walking into any sales call with a degree of certainty that the outcome will be in your favor. It means having a spirit about you that is easily contagious – a spirit that your customer can catch, and buy.

- **Total preparation is the secret sauce of assertiveness.** This must include customer-focused, pre-call planning as well as creating the objective, the proposed outcome, for a sales call. Most salespeople make the fatal mistake of preparing in terms of themselves (product knowledge, literature, business cards, blah, blah). The reality of total preparation means preparing in terms of the customer FIRST. Their needs, their desires, and their anticipated positive outcomes – their win. If these elements are not an integral part of your preparation, you will lose to someone who has them.

- **The assertive equation must also contain undeniable value in favor of the customer.** This is not just part of preparation, this is also part of the relationships you have built with other customers who are willing to testify on your behalf, and other proof that you have (hopefully in video format) that a prospective customer can relate to, believe in, and purchase as a result of.

REALITY: It's not about changing your beliefs, it's about strengthening your beliefs. It's not about changing your attitude, it's about building your attitude. It's not about changing your preparation, it's about intensifying your preparation. It's not about adding value, it's about delivering perceived value.

BIGGER REALITY: When you have mastered *belief, attitude, preparation,* and *value* as I have just defined them, then and only then, can assertiveness and assertive selling *begin* to take place.

BIGGEST REALITY: Incremental growth in belief, attitude, preparation, and value offered will lead to assertive sales calls and an increase in sales.

YOUR STATURE IS THE GLUE: Your professional look, your quiet self-confidence, your surety of knowledge and information that can help your customer, your past history of success, your possession of undeniable proof, and your assertive ability to ask your customers to be responsible to their customers and their employees. (Responsibility is an acceptable (and assertive) form of accountability). No customer wants to be *accountable* to a sales rep – but EVERY customer has a MISSION to be *responsible* to his or her customers and co-workers.

When you combine your belief, your attitude, your preparation, your value, and your assertiveness, the outcome is predictable: It's more sales.

Are you passive, aggressive, or assertive? Only one way wins.

The answer is "assertive." It's the best strategy for engaging, establishing control, proving value, creating a buying atmosphere, and forging a relationship.

I define assertiveness as a state of mind and a state of preparation PRIOR to implementation in a sales call.

The two remaining parts of assertiveness are:

1. **The sales presentation itself.**
2. **The follow-up to the sales call.**

Interesting that the sales call, the actual presentation, does not require the same amount of assertiveness as the sales follow-up. It's way more difficult to re-engage a prospect and chase down a decision.

However, if you're a great salesperson, an assertive salesperson, follow-up may not be necessary because you have asserted your way to the sale during the presentation.

THE PRESENTATION: When you get in front of a prospective customer, it is imperative that you look impressive and sound impressive. You know the old saying, "You never have a second chance to make a first impression." You must start in a positive position in order to create a positive outcome.

Assertiveness begins with your eye contact, smile, and handshake. These actions establish you in the mind of the prospect as a person who is both self-assured and happy.

You take a relaxed seat. You accept anything that is offered to you in the way of water or coffee. You put yourself in the lean-forward position. Any tools or equipment you need to make your presentation are in front of you and ready to go. And you immediately begin by discussing anything other than your business and their business.

You begin the business of making friends. You begin the business of creating mutual smiles. You begin talking about them in a way that lets them know you've done your preparation and your homework. At any moment you can begin to discuss their needs, however you prefer to discuss their family or their personal interests first.

The segue from rapport building to business discussion requires an assertive thought process. There's no formula, but there is a feeling. The salesperson's responsibility is to feel when it's right to move forward, and then have the assertive courage to do it.

Assertive presentations start with questions, offer unchallengeable proof in the middle, and end with a customer commitment that you have earned.

BEWARE and BE AWARE: Whoever you're calling on wants to know what's new and what the trends are in THEIR business. If you are able to deliver those during your presentation, I guarantee you'll develop a value-based relationship, and have the full attention of the buyer.

Harnessing the power of "assertive" in a sales presentation:

The assertive presentation challenges you, the salesperson, to bring forth a combination of your knowledge as it relates to their needs as well as a durability to connect both verbally and nonverbally with the person or the group you're addressing.

You'll know your assertive strategy is working when the customer or the prospective customer begins asking questions to get a deeper understanding about your product or service. This changes monologue to dialogue but also creates the power of engagement, or should I say *assertive engagement.*

At some point you have to complete the transaction. This means either asking for the sale (an okay part of the assertive process), or using some secondary means to confirm the sale (like scheduling delivery or installation).

Commitment to the order is where the rubber meets the road. If you get the order, it means you've done an assertively great job. If you don't get it, it means you have to lapse into assertive follow-up mode. Here's how…

THE FOLLOW UP: Assertive follow-up will become permissible if asked for, and agreed upon, in advance.

Here's how: "Mr. Jones, what's the best way for me to stay in touch with you?" "What's your preferred method of communication?" "Is there anyone else I should 'cc' in our communications?" "May I send you an occasional text?"

These are permission-based questions that tell you where you are in the relationship. If you get a cell phone number and you're permitted to send an occasional text, it means your relationship has reached a solid position.

WHERE'S THE VALUE? If I ask for a "follow-up" appointment, I'll no doubt get some vague runaround. BUT if I offer to come back with some valuable information about his or her business or job function, I'm certain to be granted that appointment.

The dialogue might go something like this, "Mr. Jones, I visit 30 or 40 businesses a month. During those visits I don't just sell, I observe. Each month I list two or three 'best practices.' In my follow-up with you, I'll need five minutes to share those practices each month. Is that fair enough?"

Heck yes! That's fair enough.

The ultimate goal beyond a sale is a trusted relationship with your customer. The path to secure that relationship begins with mastering the principles of assertiveness and then putting them into practice.

Your offer to help the customer with his or her business, and his or her job function, will not just endear you, it will also create the basis of a solid relationship. A value-based relationship.

One where assertiveness is actually acceptable.

The by-product of assertiveness is more sales.

Jeffrey Gitomer

MANIFESTO
Sales Meeting Preparation

Use the 3X process...
LinkedIn – Google – Noodle

1. Study the person and the company on LinkedIn.

2. Study the person and the company on Google.

3. Noodle and prepare three things:

   the questions you are going to ask,

   the ideas you're going to bring,

   the strategy for the meeting.

Bring IDEAS and QUESTIONS, NOT slides and sales pitches.

It's not the close.
It's the open.

Can't close a sale?

It's not because you need closing skills. It's because you need selling skills. Or better stated, relationship-building skills, questioning skills, and communication skills.

Every salesperson wants to know how to "close a sale." Even more want to know why they can't close some specific sale. They write me, they call me, they get frustrated, they buy books on the subject, they try, they get rejected, they get stalled, and of course they get lied to by their prospects.

In short, they (you) can't complete the sale.

Here's a clue: Forget closing tactics. They're worn. They're awkward. They're manipulative. And they don't put you in a very "professional" light.

Here's a bigger clue: What you have failed to uncover is the prospect's motive to buy what you're selling.

Here's the biggest clue: You're looking for a tactic when what you really need is a better strategy.

Here are 4.5 self-evaluations and idea-generators that will put your inability to close in the proper perspective.

1. Start with questions that make the prospect consider new information:

- Question them about the specific value of what you sell.
- Ask them what happened the last time they purchased what you sell.
- Ask them how a purchase will impact their profit or productivity.

2. Look at the way you present your product or service:

- Is there room for more interaction and feedback?
- Are there times in your (boring) presentation for the prospect to talk?
- What percent of the time does the prospect talk?
- How compelling is your message?
- How polished are your presentation skills?

3. Ask questions that make the prospect look good:

- Ask for their opinion.
- Ask for their feelings.
- Ask for their expertise.
- Ask for the benefit of their experience.

4. Ask for the order in a way that's "assumptive" rather than "cornering."

Ask: Assuming we pass this test today, Mr. Jones, when would be the perfect time to begin (deliver)?

4.5 Keep in mind that when your prospect is NOT talking, he or she is formulating impressions and opinions of you and what you sell.

In effect, they are deciding yes or no while you talk.

The more you let THEM talk, the easier it will be to get those feelings and impressions revealed.

Look at it this way. If you talk, you're selling. If they're talking they're selling themselves.

If you still insist on a "close" try this one: "Mr. Jones, Is there anything else you need to know before I enter your order?" The prospect will say "no" and you respond, "GREAT!"

The point of this lesson is: Not being able to close is NOT a problem. It's a symptom. The problem is: you have presented poorly or you have created barriers, or you haven't uncovered the motives to buy, or all three.

My bet? All three.

If "not closing" is a symptom, you have to look at your selling process from the beginning to find out where the problems or barriers are. If you do, you'll find out where the opportunities are to solidify a purchase BEFORE you get to the closing of the presentation.

It seems so logical to complete a sale *during* the presentation rather than the end. Why then, doesn't everyone do this?

One reason, is that it takes more preparation, more personalized information, more self-study before the presentation. Another is because many of the people who teach sales are still stuck in the 70's.

But by far, the biggest reason is that you, the supposed master salesperson, are unwilling to change your backward pattern of: gain rapport, probe, present, overcome, and close. As long as you feel the need to close you will be stuck there.

Maybe if you took a different view. One where you measured success from the front of the sales process rather than the end. Walk in. Tell the prospect that you feel he should buy from you and that you'll make a presentation to confirm it. Then tell the prospect, "If at any time during my talk you decide NOT to buy, just ring this bell (gong) – if you don't ring, I expect at the end you'll sign the contract. Is that fair enough?"

As far-fetched as this may sound to you, I ASSURE you that it beats trying to "close" times 100. Stop thinking, "Close" and establish a strategy throughout your presentation that generates a "buy."

If your "open" isn't compelling, then your "closing" will be elusive.

"Why They Buy" an answer every salesperson needs.

"Why do they buy?" is a thousand times more important than "How do I sell?" No, let me correct that… it's one million times more important than "How do I sell?" No, let me correct that… it's one billion times more important than "How do I sell?" Get the picture?

I have just spent three days in our studio interviewing the customers of my customers asking them "why they buy." And the answers are a combination of common sense, startling information, overlooked issues, and incredible opportunity.

It never ceases to amaze me that companies will spend thousands of hours and millions of dollars teaching people "how to sell," and not one minute or not ten dollars on "why they buy." And "why they buy" is all that matters.

You may think you know why they buy, but you probably don't do anything about it. Proof? Let me share with you the early warning signals that you may not have a clue as to why they buy.

1. You get price objections.

2. You have to send bids or proposals.

3. They claim to be satisfied with their present supplier.

4. No one will return your call.

4.5 You are complaining that the economy is slow.

If these sound familiar to you, you may be in the big club.

I am going to present a collection of elements as to why customers buy. They are in no particular order, but they are valid reasons that were given to me straight from the mouths of customers from every type of business.

1. I like my sales rep.

NOTE WELL: Liking is the single most powerful element in a sales relationship. I got a quote the other day from someone claiming to be a sales expert. It started out saying, "Your customer does not have to like you, but he does have to trust you." What an idiot. Can you imagine the CEO of the company when making a buying decision, saying, "I trusted that guy, but I sure didn't like him." Like leads to trust. Trust leads to buying. Buying leads to relationship. That's not the life cycle, that's the *like* cycle of sales.

2. I understand what I am buying.

3. I perceive a difference in the person and the company that I am buying from.

4. I perceive a value in the product that I am purchasing.

5. I believe my sales rep.

6. I have confidence in my sales rep.

7. I trust my sales rep.

8. I am comfortable with my sales rep.

9. I feel that there is a fit of my needs and his/her product or service.

10. The price seems fair, but it's not necessarily the lowest.

11. I perceive that this product or service will increase my productivity.

12. I perceive that this product or service will increase my profit.

12.5 I perceive that my salesperson is trying to help me build my business in order to earn his. My salesperson is a valuable resource to me.

Well, there's a few reasons to get your thought process going. If you discover yours, selling will be a snap. Go, do, now!

"Jeffrey," you whine. "Tell me how!"

OK, Here's exactly what to do.

1. Call six of your best customers.

2. Invite them to a seminar about how to build THEIR business.

3. Serve GREAT food.

4. Tell them that there are also 15-20 minutes worth of questions you want to ask them about how to strengthen your relationship.

5. **Craft six questions about how you meet their needs and what they look for in a vendor/partner. Ask "what else…"**

6. **RECORD the session. Video is best, but audio will do.**

6.5 **Listen to the recording 100 times.**

I have given you some answers as to why customers buy. But the bigger question is: Why do YOUR customers buy? Think you know? Want a cold slap in the face? YOU'VE NEVER EVEN ASKED THEM!

It amazes me that this answer is so obvious, yet so overlooked.

Understanding, recognizing and uncovering the prospect's or the customer's "motive" … Why they buy.

Salespeople have sales presentations, sales pitches, and slide decks. Customers have buying motives, needs, and desires. Oftentimes these "motives to buy" are never uncovered, because the salesperson is concentrating on their pitch rather than the customer's reasons for buying. This is the biggest mistake salespeople make while they're in a presentation. It's not "tell" until they're bored to death, it's "ask" until you uncover their primary reason for wanting to buy, and then harmonizing to be certain they buy from you. Here are their reasons for buying…

The customer's prime motive may be…

Their story

Their need

Their want

Their desire to win

Their desire to own

Their desire to solve or resolve

Their desire to recover

Their passion

Their fear

Their greed

Their vanity

Their desire to impress

Their peace of mind

Their desired outcome

Need to change vendors

Need better service

Need ease of connection

Need better speed of response

Need better quality of goods

Need better people to help

.5 asking WHY after they state their motive to determine if there's a deeper one.

NOTE WELL: You will NEVER get these answers while giving your sales pitch. People don't care what you do, or what you sell, unless they **perceive** it helps them. The way you ask questions will uncover these circumstances – THEN, the way you explain your business and product determines the buying interest you create – ask it and say it in terms of the prospect, not tell it in terms of you.

Who is taking responsibility around here? Nobody!

With all the dumb laws on the books these days, you'd think that they'd have one smart one for *taking responsibility.*

Wouldn't it be cool if every politician was not allowed to blame anybody else, and had to take responsibility for his or her own actions and results. Well, the same is true in sales.

I'm pretty sick of salespeople still telling me that, "The guy said he wasn't interested." "The guy is happy with his present supplier." "The guy won't set an appointment with me." And my all-time favorite, "The guy wouldn't return my call."

As you read them, they seem kind of lame don't they? Wait, are they lame or are they pathetic excuses for poor salesmanship, poor preparation, lack of ability to transfer a passionate message, lack of belief in your own product or company, lack of perceived value, inability to differentiate yourself from your competitor, and most important, lack of proof?

Whether you're in politics or sales the burden is the same: take responsibility for all that happens. And if it's not happening in the best way possible, take responsibility to make it happen in a better way.

It's funny how you can picture responsibility and blame in terms of a politician. I mean, come on. Can you imagine a politician saying that we didn't get the bill passed, and it was all my fault. Could you ever imagine that in your lifetime?

That's why I want taking responsibility to be a law. If it was a law, they would be forced to do it. Forced to tell the truth. Forced to admit their shortcomings. And forced to go back into the battleground, and return with a winning result.

Aren't you sick of blaming? Aren't you sick of politicians blaming each other ad nauseam for what the other guy didn't do. Isn't there some biblical phrase that begins, "Let he who is without sin cast the first stone"? I think if it were law, there would be a lot less stone casting, and a lot more people taking responsibility for making something happen.

Let's get back to the objection of not getting your call returned. When I hear a salesperson say, "The guy wouldn't return my call," I really want to punch somebody in the face (gently).

Let's take a look at the real reasons someone won't return your call, and maybe that will help you understand the difference between blaming and taking responsibility:

1. **The message you left had no value.**

2. **The customer has no intention of buying from you, just doesn't want to tell you.**

3. **The customer is not ready to buy yet and was too busy with their stuff to deal with you and your stuff.**

4. **The customer does not consider you a value provider, and is out there looking for one.**

5. **The customer does not perceive you as being genuine.**

6. **You are unaware of the customer's motive to buy, and as a result have a hard time perceiving what their urgency is. Better stated: You don't know why or when they intend to purchase.**

7. **The customer is still shopping.**

8. **You failed to connect emotionally or intellectually with the customer, and they would rather not do business with you.**

9. **You failed to offer enough proof to eliminate risk, and create peace of mind.**

9.5 **The customer has decided to buy from someone else, and feels no sense of obligation to call you.**

Those are accurate descriptions of some of the real reasons why. "The guy would not return my call" is not a problem, it's a symptom. "Why" the guy would not return my call, is the issue. Because if I can find out why, and correct it then more, if not all of my calls, will begin to be returned. Wow, what a concept.

The new way of starting your conversation might be, "I'm going to uncover my customer's intentions and motives for purchase, I'm going to share with him or her how they produce more and profit more after purchase, and I'm going to bring in several of our existing customers who will do video testimonials to corroborate my claims."

The "taking responsibility law" could revolutionize this country. I mean, can you imagine a politician actually having to tell the truth instead of blaming something or someone else?

For the past hundred years, it's been the same in sales. Salespeople and sales trainers conveniently called reasons for not buying, or not communicating, "objections." Thereby shifting the blame to the customer.

The reality is, there are no objections. There are barriers. There are symptoms. There are circumstances. But there are no objections. And all of those barriers, symptoms, and circumstances would disappear if the salesperson would only take responsibility, study the outcome, and implement a better way.

Or you can just blame and whine.

Like a politician.

AFTER the transaction, phone call, voice mail, email, product delivery, or the sales call is over, your prospect or customer will say one of 5 things about you...

Something GREAT
Something GOOD
NOTHING
Something BAD
Something REAL BAD

and YOU CHOOSE WHAT IT IS THAT THEY SAY.

Your actions, your words, and/or your deeds determine the customer's or prospect's reaction.

It's amazing to me that salespeople don't understand how much of their own outcomes and destiny they (you) control.

Jeffrey Gitomer

It's Not Rocket Science – It's Rocket Fuel.

The "Pipeline of Success."

Aren't making enough sales?
Your numbers will tell you why.

The "Numbers" it takes to make your number.

NOTE: These are not just sales numbers, they're sales ACTIVITY numbers way beyond the sales cycle. They represent the complete salesperson Manifesto numbers to crush quota and build both income and wealth.

- I need _____ sales to make my weekly goal.
- I need a weekly dollar sales volume of $ _____.
- I need a monthly dollar sales volume of $ _____.
- My closing average is _____ % (don't lie).
- I need to see ____ prospects a week to reach my goal.
- I need ____ new leads a week from my company.
- I need ____ new leads a week from my activities.
- I must spend ____ hours a week generating new leads.

- I need _____ solid appointments in the morning.
- I need _____ solid appointments in the afternoon.
- I must make _____ follow-ups per day.
- I must make _____ mailouts per day (to new contacts).
- I need _____ total prospects in my pipeline (backlog).
- I must draft _____ proposals/contracts per day.
- I must make _____ sale(s) per day.
- I must get _____ % reorders.
- I need to attend _____ networking events per month.
- Become an active member of _____ associations/clubs.
- I must spend _____ minutes a day on my attitude.
- I must spend _____ minutes a day reading.
- I must spend _____ minutes a day learning new things.
- I must spend _____ minutes a day on sales education.
- I must spend _____ minutes a day on one major goal.
- I must spend _____ minutes a day on my success.

Please fill in these numbers and compare them to your real numbers – fill in the number gaps and the hours between what you're doing to what you need to be doing. Allocate time to make the numbers a reality. Convert the "gaps" into action, and watch sales and income GROW.

And…be prepared to do business at all times…

- **Perfect positive attitude**

- **Personal awareness of opportunity**

- **Ideas prepared in advance**

- **Questions you must ask prepared in advance**

- **Memorable business cards**

- **Perfect personal commercial**

- **Testimonials that overcome objections**

Note Well:

While you are preparing for the customer, the customer is preparing for YOU. Get GOOGLE-able, or lose to someone that is.

Becoming referable is a matter of earning, not asking.

A good friend gave me a book about building your business through referrals. The author believes, "The best marketing strategy is to be referable." He is correct. He writes, "Refer-ability means that your very best clients and customers are continually cloning themselves – continually introducing you to those like themselves or better than themselves."

According to the author, your refer-ability depends upon four habits:

1. **Show up on time.**

2. **Do what you say.**

3. **Finish what you start.**

4. **Say *please* and *thank you*.**

Could being referable be that simple? The author asserts that these four habits convey respect and appreciation toward the customer. He says, if you're arrogant or erratic, you won't be referred, no matter how talented or charming you are. He says if you're not getting enough referrals, cultivate the four habits. He is partially right. Very partially.

I say his four elements DO NOT create refer-ability – his four elements are a GIVEN in any business relationship. To be referable, you have to go WAY BEYOND showing up on time and delivering what you promise.

Those habits may have worked in 1955, when *Happy Days* was in full swing, but becoming referable and earning referrals in today's times (unhappy days) are far more complex.

In my experience, I have found that a referral is earned, not asked for. When you ask for one, you immediately put your relationship in an awkward position, especially if the customer is reluctant to give you one, and you keep pestering him or her.

Here's why: The one-word definition of referral is *risk*.

When someone gives you a referral, it means they are willing to risk their relationship with the referred person or company. They have enough trust and faith in you to perform in an exemplary manner, and not jeopardize their existing friendship or business relationship.

Once you understand the definition of a referral and realize how delicate, yet powerful, it is – you at once realize why you get them (or not) – and that you must become risk free in order to earn them.

Referrals are awkward to "ask for," and often create discomfort on the part of the customer.

Here are the elements that breed proactive referrals:

1. Be likeable. This is the first prerequisite. Without a friendly relationship, there is no need to go further.

2. Be reliable. The company, the product, the service, AND you, must be "best," and "there when needed."

3. The customer considers you an expert in your field. To be referable, you must have an expertise that breeds customer confidence.

4. They trust you. The customer is CERTAIN that you will do everything in the referred party's best interest, like you have with theirs.

5. You have a track record of performance. You have already done the same thing with the customer and they're comfortable that you can repeat the performance.

5.5 They consider you valuable – a resource, not a salesman. Not just, "do what you say." There's no real value there. I mean, provide value to the customer beyond your product and service. Helping the customer to profit more, produce more, or some other form of value, either attached to your product or not. Not value in terms of you, value in terms of the customer.

And there are telltale signs – clues that you "qualify" for a referral:

REFERRAL CLUE: Your phone calls are returned. This means there was a purpose, a value, or a friendship reason. Returned calls connote respect for who you are.

REFERRAL CLUE: You get reorders. This means they WANT to do business with you, and they LIKE to do business with you.

REFERRAL CLUE: There are no problems with service issues. Your interactions are smooth and your execution is flawless.

REFERRAL CLUE: They accept your lunch invitation. And the conversation is more personal than business.

Here's the secret: If the one-word definition of referral is "risk," then you must be risk free – or at least risk tolerable.

Here's the strategy that will work 100% of the time: Give your customer a referral FIRST. It will not only blow them away, they will become an advocate on your referral team.

Here's the report card: The referral you got turned into a sale.

Free Git Bit... If you want more information on the value of a referral, go to www.gitomer.com, register if you're a first time visitor, and enter REFERRAL in the GitBit box.

Don't ask me, ask yourself! Questioning deep.

I get emails, posts and even letters with questions. Salespeople needing HELP. Salespeople wanting that instant answer.

Well here's my question back to you. What are the most important questions to ask YOURSELF? That's right – for the REAL answers you need, don't ask me – ask yourself.

Here are 54.5 critical sales, career, service, loyalty, online, and personal development questions that are guaranteed to make you think, squirm, say "ouch," and maybe even take action.

INSTRUCTIONS: Read each one, pause, think, circle the numbers that need immediate attention or further thought.

1. **What are the five most important goals for me to achieve this year?**

2. **What is my plan for each?**

3. **Why am I watching Netflix instead of working on my 5 major goals?**

4. **What would happen if I lost two of my top ten customers?**

5. **What am I doing to prevent that loss?**

6. **How often am I in front of my customers?**

7. Suppose my competition was in front of my customer once a day with something of value, and all I had was literature about me?

8. What will my website do that will make my customers buy something?

9. What will my website do that will make my customers return?

10. What does my website look like compared to my competition?

11. Do they wish they had mine or do I wish I had theirs? Or do they both suck?

12. How easy is it to do business with me?

13. Am I available to my customers 24.7.365?

14. What's my plan to get there?

15. How much do I hate a computer that answers the phone?

16. Does my company have a computer that answers the phone?

17. What am I thinking?

18. How friendly are the employees at my company?

19. How friendly am I?

20. How's my attitude?

21. Do I try to do one positive mental attitude building exercise a day?

22. What value am I bringing to my customer beyond my product and service?

23. How am I helping my customers build their business?

24. What separates me from my competition in the eyes of a customer?

25. What am I doing to earn my customer's loyalty?

26. How vulnerable am I to our competition?

27. How vulnerable am I to a price reduction from a competitor?

28. Will all my best employees or co-workers be here at the end of the year?

29. Why will some customers leave?

30. What am I "known" for?

31. What am I recognized as being "the BEST" at?

32. How excellent are my selling skills?

33. What questions am I asking my prospects and customers that my competition is not asking?

34. Why did the last five prospects say no?

35. What am I doing about it?

36. Why did the last five prospects say yes?

37. How am I building on that?

38. What does my voicemail say?

39. Is my voicemail message smart or dumb?

40. How many hours of TV a day do I watch?

41. How many hours would that be per year? (OUCH!)

42. How many of those hours are helping me succeed?

43. How many books on creativity have I read in the last 12 months?

44. How many books on sales or service have I read in the last 12 months?

45. How many books have I read in the past 12 months?

46. How many self-help podcasts have I listened to in the car last week?

47. How much time am I devoting to learning?

48. How much time am I investing in promoting and positioning my business?

49. How much am I spending to improve my image?

50. What do the leaders in my industry say about me?

51. How many people are spreading my "word" for me?

52. What's my plan to double my income over the next three years?

53. What will I need to learn to get it? What will I have to give up to get it?

54. How much do I love what I do?

54.5 (My question to you) If you don't love it, why are you doing it?

Free Git人Bit...Want a great list of books that will build your success library – and your success if you read them? Go to www.gitomer.com – register if you're a first time user, and enter the words SALES PILLS in the GitBit box.

These questions beg answers.
Answer them all, as truthfully as you can, in writing, and the Manifesto will become clear, and so will the actions you need to take to rise to success.

Manifesto Mastery

Make all decisions
based on the person you
seek to become.

Jeffrey Gitomer
KING of SALES

You gotta love what you do.
If you don't love it, you'll never
really succeed at it.

Jeffrey Gitomer
KING of SALES

It's all about the informed, the intended, the inspired, the Manifesto you.

The (non-secret) formula to make this happen is…

The daily YOU!

CHALLENGE YOURSELF DAILY

Post your goals on your bathroom mirror.

EDUCATE YOURSELF DAILY

15 minutes in the morning makes you a world-class expert in 5 years.

INTEND TO IMPROVE DAILY

The biggest room in your home is the room for improvement. Commit to learning something new each day.

INTEND TO FOLLOW THROUGH DAILY

Following up is simply asking for money. Following through makes the sale, delivers the product or service, and forges the value-based relationship after **the sale.**

AFFIRM YOURSELF DAILY

What are your ten affirmations?

Where are they? And when do you say them?

REWARD YOURSELF DAILY

A walk, a cookie, a small reminder you worked hard and achieved.

INSPIRE YOURSELF EVERY DAY

Read something in the morning or write something in the morning that sets your mind on fire, and lights the candle under your ass.

INTEND TO BE POSITIVE

Read one page from the Yes! Attitude book every day.

THE DAILY SALES MANIFESTO

Get better at ONE Manifesto element every day.

Simple self-disciplines repeated over time will lead to success.

Small errors in judgment repeated over time will lead to failure.

Jim Rohn

What's in a nickname? Ask Wayne Gretzky.

Gaining sales mastery has little to do with "closing the sale." And for your own success, ignore anyone who tells you otherwise. If you go to a seminar and the person leading it says, "These are the five best closes…" – get up and walk out.

People don't want to be "closed." They want to feel great about "buying."

What's the answer then?

Closing is selling. People don't like to be sold, but they love to buy™. Asking creates dialog and answers. Ask before you tell.

That's a sales mastery point.

How do you become a master salesperson? And – how do you become a master salesperson at a time when in many industries, sales couldn't be worse?

The answer lies in two strategic areas that are closely tied to one another. The first is "skill mastery" in the 10.5 critical elements of the sale. And the second is "study" or forever remain a student of that which you seek to master.

Without getting into a dissertation as to "why" these are the strategies, let me just present them and you can judge for yourself (you will anyway). At the end, "why" will be evident, or you're in the wrong profession.

If you want to make sales when no one else can, the only way you can do it is if you are the "master." Once you are the master, it doesn't matter what the economic conditions are. Once you are the master, it doesn't matter what your market is doing. You are the master.

When Wayne Gretzky played hockey for the Edmonton Oilers they called him "The Great One." Then he was traded to the LA Kings – did they call him "The Good One" there? No, he was still called The Great One. Then he went to the St. Louis Blues – did they call him "The Good One" there? No – still The Great One. Finally he was traded to the NY Rangers. What do you think they called him there? The Great One.

Take the lesson:
When you're The Great One,
no matter what team you play for,
you're still The Great One.

Personal things you can do for yourself without anyone's approval

1. Exercise daily.

2. Eliminate sugar from your diet.

3. Take vitamin and herbal supplements.

4. Get up 1 hour earlier than everyone else.

5. Read about your mind and your career… for 30 minutes a day.

6. Take responsibility for your actions… every hour of every day.

7. Make the last call every day.

8. Post your goals on your bathroom mirror.

9. Always have something good to say about someone else.

10. Do the things that are uncomfortable…they are usually on the *edge*.

10.5

Don't let anyone or anything discourage you, no matter what.

Understanding and implementing MANIFESTO Growth Mastery

Make all decisions based on the person you want to become – OPPORTUNITY.

For the past 25 years, I wake up in the morning and I immediately do one of five things – sometimes all five. Write, read, prepare, think, create.

It's a fraction…

$$\frac{\textbf{Write, Read, Prepare}}{\textbf{Think, Create}}$$

and it has helped me BECOME who I am, and will help me achieve who I still strive to become.

MANIFESTO SALES REALITY CHECK:

In sales you have ONE CHANCE.
One chance to engage,
One chance to build rapport,
One chance to connect,
One chance to be believable,
One chance to be trustworthy,
One chance to meet with the
real decision-maker.
One chance to differentiate yourself,
One chance to prove your value,
and one chance to ask for
(or better, confirm) the sale.

Don't "take a chance."
Do "take advantage of your
ONE chance."

Jeffrey Gitomer

The 12.5 Values of a Manifesto Sales Professional

1. The value of creating a difference between you and the competition

The biggest difference is the difference they perceive in YOU!

2. The value of knowing the difference between satisfied and loyal

Satisfied customers buy anywhere. Loyal customers stay, fight for you, and refer.

3. The value of your ability to speak and be compelling

If your sales message is boring they pass. If it's compelling, they want to buy.

4. The value of knowing everything or being too busy

All the information you need to succeed already exists. You may not be exposing yourself to it.

5. The value of establishing a friendly relationship

All things being equal, people want to do business with their friends.

All things being not quite so equal, people still want to do business with their friends.

6. The value of your humor

If you can make 'em laugh, you can make 'em buy. Study humor.

7. The value of creativity

Your key to being perceived as different lies in your creativity.

Creativity can be learned.

8. The value of asking for the sale

It's so simple, no one does it.

9. The value of your belief in yourself

To make a sale, you gotta believe you work for the greatest company in the world,

you gotta believe you have the greatest products and services in the world,

you gotta believe you're the greatest person in the world.

Three key words, *you gotta believe*.

10. The value of being prepared

Most salespeople are half prepared.

They know everything about themselves, they know nothing about their prospect.

11. The value of not whining

You may be the greatest – but if you whine, no one will like or respect you.

12. The value of an apple a day

An hour of learning a day will make you a world-class expert at anything in 5 years.

12.5 The value of a YES! Attitude

Attitude is EVERYTHING.

You become what you think about.

Your attitude is at the core of every action you take.

Attract with message, engage with value, connect with emotion, and sell with proof.

Jeffrey Gitomer
KING of SALES

In sales, it's not who you know, in sales it's who knows YOU!

Jeffrey Gitomer
KING of SALES

Master The Big 8.5 Elements of Positioning

The art of becoming a valued authority

1. **Getting in print – a story about you**
   (using your own PR)
2. **Being published**
   (writing)
3. **Speaking in public**
   (presumed leader)
4. **Using the internet to communicate value**
   (help them profit first)
5. **Taking an active role in your trade association**
   (networking)
6. **Being noticeably different**
   (risking in all aspects of writing, speaking, and posting)
7. **Making value attraction a consistent activity**
   (offering something more that others desire)
8. **Adding differentiation**
   (voice mail, proposal, business card)

8.5 **Let others sell for you**
   (testimonial proof both socially and face-to-face.
   Prospects will believe others like themselves, not you)

Read It and Reap

The real success, fulfillment, and money elements of making Dominant Sales Manifesto YOUR reality

- **Dominate Yourself First.** Be your BEST and give your BEST at all times. You can never give your best to others unless and until you are the best you can be for yourself FIRST.

- **Your Attitude and your Belief precede Domination.** Study Yes! Attitude DAILY. Deepen your belief in company, product and self.

- **The Friendly Factor.** It costs no extra money to be friendly.

- **Give Value First.** The backbone of promotion AND attraction. Give without expectation of return and you win forever.

- **Promote Yourself and Your Message with Your Own PODCAST.** It's time to take the next step into next-level dominance. Listen to and subscribe to *Sell or Die* to understand why and how.

- **Position yourself as a Dominator.** Develop a massive social platform AND social presence. Social is not an option – it's your first and lasting impression. Create impeccable social reputation.

- **Promote Yourself with Value, NOT Advertising.** Post messages worth reading, learning from, and sharing. Create consistent value-based social postings.

- **Learn the Science of Social Selling.** Create value-based attraction.

- **Secure Consistent Social Proof of Your Product and You.**

- **Have Impressive Google-ability.** Google yourself every day until you love the results.

- **The Depth of Your Social Platform Creates your Social Relevance.** Be relevant, or lose to someone who is.

ASSESS YOURSELF – free 5 Question Manifesto Assessment (www.thesalesmanifesto.com/assessment).

Attract with message, engage with value, connect with emotion, and sell with proof.

Jeffrey Gitomer
KING of SALES

Fifty Shades of Sales. Putting emotion first, and price second.

It seems society is loosening up. The Internet, music, movies, book titles, TV, and texting have created an openness revolution not matched since the 60's.

And with the recent explosion in popularity (and sales) of the trilogy, *Fifty Shades of Gray,* it seemed to me that the world of sales needs to loosen up in the same way.

Not THAT kind of loose. Shheeeese.

It's not that selling is particularly sexy, or erotic – but it's definitely emotional. You, the salesperson, enter the sale full of emotion, and do your best to transfer your emotion to the prospect – and even capture their emotion. Once there is emotional transfer and emotional agreement, the likelihood of a sale is much higher than a "professional" or "manipulative" approach or presentation.

To understand the concept of Fifty Shades of Sales more fully, you have to be aware of the way that sales are made. *The sale is made emotionally, and justified logically.*

You have made a significant emotional investment in the sale. Your emotions rise and fall with the decisions of other people. Sometimes you score. Sometimes you don't. But either way, there's an overflow of emotional energy.

If you're looking to GROW your own business or sales career, you have to CROW your own business and your persona with value messages that help others grow and crow theirs.

Jeffrey Gitomer
KING of SALES

Customers are also extremely emotional – before they take ownership (need, desire), as you're presenting (risk, doubt, caution), when they take ownership (pride, gratification), and when something goes wrong (fear, anger).

Even price buyers express the (emotional) need, want, or desire to own something. And after the emotional decision is made – THEN they logically hunt down, justify, or decide on the affordability of the price.

Your challenge is to harness prospect-emotion and create enough of a positive atmosphere and perceived value to purchase from you.

GREAT NEWS: Your shades of gray, er sales, are within your total control.

Here are the emotional elements and actions that will create a buying atmosphere:

- **Asking emotional questions about their experience and wisdom.**
- **Your passionate compelling presentation.**
- **Your personal, transferrable, and consistent enthusiasm.**
- **Attitude that comes from your heart.**
- **Serving because you love to serve.**
- **Belief that the customer is better off having purchased from you – and believing that in your heart – not your head.**
- **Connecting personally and building meaningful rapport.**

- Uncovering and understanding the motive (or motives) of the customer to buy.

- Making certain that your value message goes beyond your price. When value exceeds price, purchase occurs.

- Wowing the customer as a regular part of your process in sales and service.

- Using an emotional video from other customers as proof of your authenticity, quality, and value.

- Reassuring the customer after they purchase.

- Becoming genuinely interested in the prospect – a classic Dale Carnegie axiom.

- Doing more than is expected – a classic Napoleon Hill axiom.

- Giving value first – a classic Jeffrey Gitomer axiom.

That's a sales list of qualities you can sink your teeth into. They're real, they create emotional engagement, and they can all be mastered over time. Below are the elements you must possess to be the master of YOUR EMOTIONAL SELF, before you can enter the sales arena with customers and prospects.

You determine your own emotion by the spoken and unspoken elements of who you are as a person:

- Your internal positive attitude

- Your smile

- Your self-confidence

- **The way you present yourself to others**
- **The way you speak to others, both in tone and words**
- **Who you seek to become as a person**
- **How you live your life**
- **How you earn respect**
- **Your peer reputation**
- **Your community reputation**
- **Your online reputation**
- **Your love of family**
- **Daily random acts of kindness**

And the shade – the degree – of emotion you put into each of these elements, will determine the outcome of your sales effort, and your relationship effort, far more times than your price, your insincere communication, or your closing tactics.

BEWARE AND BE AWARE: Closing the sale, finding the pain and manipulation, and closing the sale, aren't in the shades of gray spectrum – they're black. Customers are smarter than that, and they see right through your phony words and process.

PRACTICE SAFE SALES. You got into sales to win, and make income beyond the safety of a salary – you'll have to take risks along the way, but do not risk ethical violation of practice or threatening your reputation based on actions.

178 Jeffrey Gitomer

The Sales Manifesto

MANIFESTO Definition of TRUSTED ADVISOR

Someone who is inside the boardroom HELPING a decision to be made. YES!

MANIFESTO Definition of SALESPERSON

Someone who is OUTSIDE the boardroom sitting on a bench waiting for a decision to be made. Ouch!

You learn by clarification of situation and opportunity. You become proficient by taking action. You master by repetition of process.

Jeffrey Gitomer
KING of SALES

Manifesto
Thoughts and Thinking

QUOTES BY OTHERS:

What are your favorite quotes, and where are they?

Do you look at them daily?

Here are the best of other people's that I have collected:

Think about them. Be inspired by them. Put them into action.

Nothing happens until a sale is made.

Red Motley

Every child should be taught to expect success.

Orison Swett Marden

Every winner has scars.

Herbert Casson

If you want others to believe in you,
you must first convince them that
you believe in yourself.

Harvey Mackay

Who can you call at 2AM?

Harvey Mackay

Be yourself, everyone else
is already taken.

Oscar Wilde

Before you try to convince
anyone else, be sure you are
convinced, and if you cannot
convince yourself, drop the subject.

John H. Patterson (founder of NCR)

You become what you think about.

Earl Nightingale

The person who stops studying merely because he has finished school is forever hopelessly doomed to mediocrity, no matter what may be his calling. The way of success is the way of continuous pursuit of knowledge.

Napoleon Hill

Instead of worrying about what people say of you, why not spend time trying to accomplish something they will admire.

Dale Carnegie

You can make more friends in two months by being interested in other people, than in two years of trying to get people interested in you.

Dale Carnegie

All the information you need to succeed
already exists, the only problem is
you're not exposing yourself to it!

Jim Rohn

Your attitude towards others
determines their attitude towards us.

Earl Nightingale

Somebody may beat me, but they are
going to have to bleed to do it.

Steve Prefontaine

Personality can open doors,
but only character can keep them open.

Elmer Leterman

Learn to enjoy every
minute of your life.

Be happy now.

Don't wait for something
outside of yourself
to make you happy
in the future.

Think how really precious is the
time you have to spend, whether
it's at work or with your family.

Every minute should be
enjoyed and savored.

Earl Nightingale

Definition of Up-sell…

Son, when their wallet is open, empty it!

MAX GITOMER

The Secret to Beat Inflation…

Son, earn more money!

MAX GITOMER

Ultimate Manifesto Success

"The only difference between where you are now, and where you'll be five years from now, are the books you'll read, the places you'll go, and the people you'll meet."

Charlie "Tremendous" Jones
MENTOR

My Manifesto morning formula...

Write, Read, Prepare

Think, Create

(I have been using this formula
DAILY for the past 25 years.
I don't know how good it's working so far,
so I'm going to keep using it
for the next 25 years – and then
that's it – I'm gonna quit.)

Jeffrey Gitomer

A Free eBook Awaits You…

How to Have Your Best DECADE Ever!

Having your best year ever is passé – I have compiled the document (based on this Manifesto) for you to have your best DECADE ever. It's not a matter of doing one thing right – or even making one thing better – it's a matter of making everything better, and mastering the manifesto elements so that you can get to BEST. Below are the elements. Go here (www.bestdecadeever.com) to get the entire eBook – it will provide a path to the Yellow Brick Road – past Oz – all the way to your bank!

1. **Define yourself.**

2. **Develop a sales mission statement.**

3. **Have a deep belief in the three critical areas of selling.**

4. **Develop greater pride in accomplishment.**

5. **You are what you eat.**

6. **Get rid of one time-waster.**

7. **Read a book every two months.**

8. **Get your (sales) pipeline full.**

9. Get your monthly sales quota met by the second week of the month.

10. Start branding yourself.

11. Get up earlier.

12. Begin capturing your thoughts and ideas in writing.

13. Give one speech.

14. Write one article your customers will read.

15. Make sales at breakfast.

16. Keep your present customers loyal to you and your company.

17. Double your testimonials.

18. Double your referrals.

19. Record your sales presentation.

20. Start every morning with attitude.

20.5 You're not alone. Create a mastermind.

This eBook will go beyond understanding today and making sales now. It will give you a firm game plan for a decade. Let me repeat the offer: Go here (www.bestdecadeever.com) to get the entire E-book – it will provide the Yellow Brick Road – past Oz – all the way to your bank! Go now.

My Manifesto Affirmations:

I DO care that I am the master of my personal development, my sales and my service. I take care of myself FIRST, so that I may best take care of others second.

I study creativity – I see things from every perspective and generate ideas for myself and others.

I am the master of the question – I get the truth (expose them) by asking questions.

I am the master of rapid response – fast or faster.

I am the master of "them communication" – they don't care about you.

I am the master of recovery – ask them, don't tell them.

I am the master of relationships – all things being equal…

I am the master of personal communication – the ezine keeps you in touch.

I am the master of networking (with customers and co-workers) – schmooze.

I am the master of milking my own cows.

I am the master of passing the baton – I delegate.

I am a master of "the sale after the sale" (wow that was cool).

I am a master of "the service after the service" (wow that was cool).

AFFIRM DOMINATION FUNDAMENTALS

- I have the attitude, I have the self-confidence, I have the swagger, I have the assertiveness – NOT the aggressiveness

- I Intend to do, not just make a goal

- I am making emotional connections

- I wake up and read and write EVERY DAY

- I post to attract, not brag

- I use post it note goals on my bathroom mirror

- I hang around achievers

- I don't just network, I get involved where you network

- I don't just attend or exhibit at the trade show – I speak there

- I join groups that can help me and others get better – I am a toastmaster

- I will buy and take courses from masters ONLINE – I will invest in myself

21.5 Unbreakable Laws of Selling
The ULTIMATE AFFIRMATIONS

Proven Actions You Must Take to Make Easier, Faster, Bigger Sales... NOW and FOREVER!

Instructions for reading: Read each law 5x, add these 5 affirmations, one at a time to each law, and then take actions.

1. **I must...**
2. **I need to...**
3. **Here are my reasons to...**
4. **I think I can...**
5. **I will...**

Add the 5 affirmations, one at a time, to each law. Then buy the book...

Unbreakable Law 1: Attract Willing Buyers

Unbreakable Law 2: Think YES!

Unbreakable Law 3: Believe Before You Succeed

Unbreakable Law 4: Employ Humor

Unbreakable Law 5: Build Your Own Brand

Unbreakable Law 6: Earn Reputation

Unbreakable Law 7: Be Assertive and Persistent

Unbreakable Law 8: Demonstrate Excellence

Unbreakable Law 9: Deliver Value First

Unbreakable Law 10: Communicate in Terms of Them

Unbreakable Law 11: Ask Before You Tell

Unbreakable Law 12: Serve Memorably

Unbreakable Law 13: Exchange Loyalty

Unbreakable Law 14: Earn Trust

Unbreakable Law 15: Utilize Voice of Customers

Unbreakable Law 16: Discover the Why

Unbreakable Law 17: Intend to Achieve

Unbreakable Law 18: Be Perceived as Different

Unbreakable Law 19: Perform Dynamically

Unbreakable Law 20: Attract, Engage, and Connect Socially

Unbreakable Law 21: Earn Without Asking

Unbreakable Law 21.5: Love It or Leave It

"When you master the laws, you will reap their rewards."

Jeffrey Gitomer

Mandatory
Manifesto Actions

- **Mandatory morning coffee with money**

- **Give referrals to get referrals**

- **Give loyalty to get loyalty**

- **Deepen relationships with consistent value offerings**

- **Earn referrals with value-first philosophy**

- **Double your time in front of people who can say YES to you**

These are the core Manifesto
elements to build your foundation
of success and wealth.
Study them. Personalize them.
And put them into daily
action – for yourself.

You can't just read this Manifesto. In order to get the message, you have to study the message, live the message, and repeat the message, the ideas and the strategies until they become ingrained in your soul.

Jeffrey Gitomer
KING of SALES

THE FUNDAMENTAL 11.5 R's of engaging, serving, WOWing, and keeping customers loyal

THE REPORT CARD of MANIFESTO SALES MASTERY

To advance past others and collect relationships, repeat business, referrals, and top-line remuneration, here are the elements defined...

11.5 R's of Selling as the Measurement

1. **Relationships (the key to growth and profit)**

2. **Reorders/Repeat business (earned through value, quality, and service)**

3. **Referrals (earn them)**

4. **Reputation (it's now visible for all to see)**

5. **Response/Responsiveness (immediate is the watchword)**

6. **Responsibility (the opposite of blame)**

7. **Resilience (react, respond, and recover)**

8. **Remuneration (pay and get paid)**

9. **Relentless (even if your ass falls off)**

10. **Resource (using them and being one)**

11. **Results (measure unsolicited referrals and profit)**

11.5 **REALITY (you are the master of your fate)**

If you do it right, you will survive.
If you do it right and right now,
you will thrive.
If you do it right, with value,
and you do it right now,
you will prosper.

Jeffrey Gitomer
KING of SALES

The Jeffrey Gitomer
Sales Manifesto
for ultimate success.

Here's the REALITY in a nutshell....

- Your YES! Attitude and personal belief put you on a mental path to success.

- Your understanding of why customers buy your product gives you sales insight.

- Your face-to-face networking gets you contacts, leads, and builds relationships.

- Your social networking builds attraction, engagement, followers, and connections.

- Your use of business social media builds your online presence, your reputation, your GoogleJuice (ranking).

- Your company website, COMBINED with your personal website, blog, YouTube channel, your social presence, and your weekly e-zine (value message from what you write) get you positioned and known in your market, on Google, and in the mind of your customer.

- Your Internet position and Google presence gets you branded and known.

- Your name gets you in the door…NOTE WELL: Your reputation precedes you, and the customer Googles you as you walk in the door.

- Your deep belief in what you sell will create emotional engagement with your prospect.

- Your creativity differentiates you from your competition.

- Your compelling presentation skills earn attention, respect, and help transfer your message.

- Your love of what you do creates a compelling, passionate message.

- Your questions emotionally engage and create rapport.

- Your questions uncover prospects motives for buying, and reveals their urgency to own what you're offering.

- Your questions get you real answers and earn respect.

- Your questions differentiate you from your competition.

- Your ideas get you listened to and talked about.

- Your ideas differentiate you and prove your value.

- Your "product pitch" is largely wasted on deaf ears and could have been found online.

- Your old-world selling tactics cost respect and business.

- Your understanding of how your product is used after purchase is the key to sale.

- Your price and proposal compares you to the rest.

- Your PERCEIVED VALUE is what gets you bought again and again.

- Your perceived value gets you bought (at your price).

- Their unspoken risk (not your price) is the real barrier.

- Your testimonials prove your worth and value (if they perceive no differentiating value, they'll compare price and buy price… from anyone).

- Once your product or service is delivered, all truth is revealed.

- Your ability to deliver beyond expectation gets you talked about and bought again.

- Your availability, ease of doing business, speed of response, and friendliness create a customer's desire beyond price to become loyal.

- Your ability to stay in touch and provide continued value creates repeat business, referrals, word-of-mouth advertising, and the law of attraction.

- Referrals, especially unsolicited, are the report card for what and how your customer thinks of you, and how they value you.

Your reputation and success are the sum total result of all these actions. And the secret to HUGE wins is the "Value First" proposition.

The main reason salespeople fail, or only reach a level of mediocrity, is that they don't concentrate on the customer's OUTCOME, they're only focused on their own INCOME.

Jeffrey Gitomer
KING of SALES

JEFFREY GITOMER
Chief Executive Salesman

Gitomer Defined (git-o-mer) n. 1. a creative, on-the-edge writer and speaker whose expertise on sales, customer loyalty, and personal development is world renowned; 2. known for presentations, seminars, and keynote addresses that are funny, insightful, and in-your-face; 3. real-world; 4. off-the-wall; 5. on the money; and 6. gives audiences information they can take out in the street one minute after the seminar is over and then they can turn it into money. He is the ruling King of Sales. See also: salesman.

AUTHOR. Jeffrey Gitomer is the author of the *New York Times* bestsellers *The Sales Bible, The Little Red Book of Selling, The Little Black Book of Connections*, and *The Little Gold Book of YES! Attitude*. Most of his books have been number one bestsellers on Amazon.com, including *Customer Satisfaction Is Worthless, Customer Loyalty Is Priceless, The Little Platinum Book of Cha-Ching, The Little Red Book of Sales Answers, The Little Green Book of Getting Your Way, The Little Platinum Book of Cha-Ching!, The Little Teal Book of Trust, Social BOOM!, The Little Book of Leadership, and the 21.5 Unbreakable Laws of Selling* and *Jeffrey Gitomer's Sales Manifesto*. Jeffrey's books have appeared on major bestseller lists more than 500 times and have sold millions of copies worldwide.

EDITOR AND ANNOTATOR of TRUTHFUL LIVING. In conjunction with The Napoleon Hill Foundation, Jeffrey was given the honor of editing and annotating Napoleon Hill's first writings. Written in 1917 these are Hill's never before seen original success thoughts.

OVER 2,500 PRESENTATIONS. Jeffrey gives public and corporate seminars, runs annual sales meetings, and conducts live and virtual training programs on selling, YES! Attitude, trust, customer loyalty, and all aspects of personal development.

BIG CORPORATE CUSTOMERS. Jeffrey's customers include Coca-Cola, US Foodservice, Caterpillar, BMW, Verizon, DELL, MacGregor Golf, Hilton, General Motors, Enterprise Rent-A-Car, NCR, IBM, Comcast Cable, Time Warner, Liberty Mutual, Wells Fargo, Blue Cross Blue Shield, Carlsberg, Mutual of Omaha, AC Nielsen, Northwestern Mutual, Church Mutual Insurance, MetLife, GlaxoSmithKline, the New York Post, and hundreds of others.

ON THE INTERNET. Jeffrey's WOW website, Gitomer.com, gets thousands of hits per week from readers and seminar attendees. His state-of-the-art presence on the Web and e-commerce ability has set the standard among peers, and has won huge praise and acceptance from customers. Jeffrey's blog, salesblog.com, is another free resource for sales and personal development information. BUSINESS SOCIAL MEDIA. Keep up with Jeffrey and his social media presence on Facebook, Twitter, LinkedIn, Instagram, Pintrest, and YouTube. New ideas, events, and special offers are posted daily. With more than one million social media followers, and more than five million YouTube views, Jeffrey has built a groundswell of attraction and engagement.

ONLINE SALES AND PERSONAL DEVELOPMENT LEARNING. Gitomer Learning Academy will help you learn more to earn much more. Gitomer Learning Academy contains real-world interactive video courses based on Jeffrey's personal sales experience and contains his full body of work in sales and personal development. The Academy has more than 500-hours of fully searchable and easily implementable sales actions and ideas to give you the answers you need, when you need them. The Academy starts with a skills-based sales assessment and then offers an interactive certification course. It is continually updated as Jeffrey records new video lessons and content. It's ongoing sales information, answers, motivation, sales reinforcement, and personal inspiration. The Academy has the ability to track, measure, and monitor progress and achievement. Gitomer Learning Academy is innovative. Gitomer Learning Academy is game-ified. Go to GitomerLearningAcademy.com – Play to Win.

SELL OR DIE PODCAST. Jeffrey Gitomer and Jennifer Gluckow share their sales and personal development knowledge in their weekly podcast, Sell or Die. In today's world of constant change there is still one constant, you're either selling or dying. Tune in on iTunes or your favorite podcast app – just search for Sell or Die.

PODCAST NETWORK TO EXPAND YOUR LEARNING. After more than 1,000,000 downloads of Sell or Die, Jeffrey, Jennifer, and Doug Branson, decided to form a podcast network to help our subscribers find additional quality information. By subscribing to the network you will continue to access the best sales and personal development information in the world.

SALES CAFFEINE. Jeffrey's weekly magazine, Sales Caffeine, is a sales wake-up call delivered every Tuesday morning to more than 250,000 subscribers, free of charge. Sales Caffeine allows Jeffrey to communicate valuable sales information, strategies, and answers to sales professionals. You can subscribe at www.salescaffeine.com.

AWARD FOR PRESENTATION EXCELLENCE. In 1997, Jeffrey was awarded the designation of Certified Speaking Professional (CSP) by the National Speakers Association. The CSP award is the association's highest earned designation.

SPEAKER HALL OF FAME. In August 2008, Jeffrey was inducted into the National Speaker Association's Speaker Hall of Fame. The designation CPAE (Counsel of Peers Award for Excellence) honors professional speakers who have reached the top echelon of performance excellence. Each candidate must demonstrate mastery in seven categories: originality of material, uniqueness of style, experience, delivery, image, professionalism, and communication. To date, only 219 of the world's greatest speakers have been inducted including Ronald Reagan, Art Linkletter, Colin Powell, Norman Vincent Peale, Earl Nightingale, and Zig Ziglar.

I give VALUE first.
I HELP other people.
I strive to be my BEST at
what I LOVE to do.
I establish LONG TERM RELATIONSHIPS
With everyone.
I have FUN –
and I do that EVERY DAY.

Jeffrey Gitomer
KING of SALES

GitomerLearningAcademy.com
Subscribe to the BEST learning experience on the planet.
Online. On demand. On the money.

GITOMERLEARNING**ACADEMY.COM**

Subscribe and Listen to

Sell or Die

The #1 Rated Sales and
Personal Development Podcast

You learn by clarification of situation and opportunity.

You become proficient by taking action.

You master by repetition of process.

Jeffrey Gitomer
KING of SALES

Bring Jeffrey Live to your sales event or annual meeting.

Make the Sales Manifesto come to life and breathe new sales ideas and inspiration into the minds and hearts of your sales team with Jeffrey's customized, in your face, funny as hell high energy performance.

Rated the number ONE Sales, Attitude, and Personal Development speaker in the world, Jeffrey delivers customized, real-world sales information that your people can take out into the streets ONE MINUTE after they hear it, and turn it into MONEY!

Call 704.333.1112 or email helpme@gitomer.com

www.gitomer.com